D1006103

THE
MYSTERIES of
HISTORY

THE
MYSTERIES
of
HISTORY

UNRAVELLING THE TRUTH
FROM THE MYTHS OF
OUR PAST

Graeme Donald

Michael O'Mara Books Limited

First published in Great Britain in 2018
by Michael O'Mara Books Limited
9 Lion Yard
Tremadoc Road
London SW4 7NQ

Copyright © Michael O'Mara Books Limited 2018

All rights reserved. You may not copy, store, distribute, transmit,
reproduce or otherwise make available this publication (or any part
of it) in any form, or by any means (electronic, digital, optical,
mechanical, photocopying, recording or otherwise), without the
prior written permission of the publisher. Any person who does any
unauthorized act in relation to this publication may be liable to
criminal prosecution and civil claims for damages.

A CIP catalogue record for this book is available from
the British Library.

Papers used by Michael O'Mara Books Limited are natural,
recyclable products made from wood grown in sustainable forests.
The manufacturing processes conform to the environmental
regulations of the country of origin.

ISBN: 978-1-78243-902-8 in hardback print format
ISBN: 978-1-78243-969-1 in ebook format

1 2 3 4 5 6 7 8 9 10

Designed and typeset by Ed Pickford
Illustrations by Greg Stevenson

Printed and bound by CPI Group (UK) Ltd, Croydon, CR0 4YY

www.mombooks.com

For Rhona – she knows why!

Contents

3. Murder Most Foul

4. Riddles of Ritual and Religion

5. Conflict and Catastrophe

Introduction

VOLTAIRE ONCE DISMISSED historians as nothing more than gossips who tease the dead, glorify the inglorious and vilify those who are worthy but unpopular with whoever is paying for the history books to be written.

And to a certain extent he was right. There are major events from history that are still presented today as a maze of conflicting disinformation and biased opinion that leave the modern reader trying to navigate their way to the truth through a rather confusing fog. When it comes to a re-examination of the reputations of prominent characters from our past, some emerge from closer scrutiny stripped of their veneer of nobility, while others, previously thought unworthy, emerge significantly less tarnished.

The biased rewriting of history includes the almost criminal fiasco that was the Charge of the Light Brigade, which had to be rebranded as a shimmering example of the unquestioning heroism of the average British soldier in order to save face, and the seemingly monstrous Dr Crippen, who was railroaded to the gallows by a young forensic scientist determined to make a name for himself. Or the real story of Elizabeth Báthory, the woman dubbed

Countess Dracula, who was far from the terrifying character she was made out to be, but rather a victim of her enormous wealth.

When writing this book, the greatest care has been taken to avoid the pitfalls of relying on biased sources so, no matter how eminent the writer of any one particular source, all dates and information have been cross-checked against others of both sympathetic and opposing opinion. That said, should any reader find an error, I would be very happy to make the correction.

Graeme Donald

1
Smoke and Mirrors

JOAN OF ARC: A FRENCH
(FLIGHT OF) FANCY

MANY ACCOUNTS OF Joan of Arc portray her as a heroine of the early fifteenth century. They tell of her leading the French armies to countless victories over the English invaders and their Burgundian allies before she was captured and burned as a witch in the marketplace of Rouen. But in fact, among other things, it seems she wasn't French, she never commanded any army or even fought in battle, and she was not executed for witchcraft. So how did such inaccuracies build to create this iconic character?

She was born in 1412 at Domrémy in Lorraine, an independent duchy not assimilated into France until 1766. Her father was Jacques Darce, his name variously presenting as Darx, Darc and even Tarce but not d'Arc, as the apostrophe was never used in fifteenth-century French names and there was no such place as Arc from which he could have hailed. Her mother was Isabelle de Vouthon, and both she and Jacques elected to be known by the surname of Romée, though it is unclear which of them, if either, had undertaken the pilgrimage to Rome to qualify for such usage. Their daughter was christened Jehannette, not Jeanne/Joan, and it was not until the nineteenth century that the epithet Jeanne d'Arc or Joan of Arc appeared through a misreading of Darc; during her alleged lifetime she was referred to as *La Pucelle*, 'The Maid'. The Romées were not of simple peasant stock; Jacques was a highly successful farmer and leading citizen who allegedly threatened to 'strangle her [Jehannette] with my own hands if she goes into France'. From that, if nothing else, we may safely assume that the people of Domrémy considered themselves to be anything but French.

Much that is told of Jehannette comes from chronicles discovered in Notre Dame in the nineteenth century, but not everyone is convinced that these documents are genuine. According to Roger Caratini, regarded by some to be one of France's most prestigious historians:

I'm very much afraid that precious little of what we French have been taught in school about Joan of Arc is true ... She was, it seems, almost entirely the creation of France's desperate need for a patriotic mascot in the nineteenth century. The country wanted a hero, the myths of the revolution were altogether too bloody, and France more or less invented the story of its patron saint. The reality is, sadly, a little different ... Joan of Arc played no role, or at best only a very minor one, in the Hundred Years War. She was not the liberator of Orléans for the simple reason that the city was never besieged. And the English had nothing to do with her death. I'm afraid it was the Inquisition and the University of

Paris that tried and sentenced her ... I'm afraid the fact of the matter is that we were the ones who killed our national hero. We may have a problem with the English, but as far as Joan's concerned, we really shouldn't.

IMAGINARY VOICES

Little interest was shown in the shadowy figure of 'Joan' – even in France – until Napoleon decided to resurrect her as a cult figure. But if she really did lead her sub-commanders to such stunning victories in the Hundred Years War, where are all the glowing testimonies from them? All we really have is a vague tale of a young woman who heard voices and 'saw things'. She is said to have claimed that her two main 'voices' were those of St Margaret of Antioch and St Catherine of Alexandria and while in her time the reality of these two was accepted, it has since been established beyond the doubt of even the most fervent hagiophile that neither in fact existed. This leaves us with a likely fictitious heroine allegedly guided by the voices of two other women who did not exist. But none of this prevented her from being canonized in 1920.

Caratini is by no means alone in thinking Joan a nineteenth-century invention or, at best, 'one of many maids who followed the army, carrying a banner on the same daily pay as an archer'. France at the time was in turmoil. Assisted by their allies, the Burgundians, the English were in control of vast swathes of the country, resulting in the French court relocating to the safety of Chinon in the Loire. If the entire legend is to be accepted at face value, then we are required to believe that an uneducated sixteen-year-old farm girl, who could barely write her own name, simply rode down to Chinon and, having unerringly picked out the Dauphin who was hiding among his own courtiers to test her, told him of her 'voices' and repeated a few prophecies before sauntering out as a battle commander. Even if the Dauphin had been daft enough to make such an appointment, is it realistic to believe that the battle-hardened troops assigned to her banner would have meekly followed, given that she knew nothing of tactics and weaponry?

Had the Maid been the stuff of her own legend, it is puzzling that the first biographical work purporting to detail her life was not written until the seventeenth century by Edmond Richer, head of the Faculty of Theology at the Sorbonne in Paris, his manuscript lying unpublished in archives until 1911. After Richer, the next to tackle the subject was Nicolas Lenglet Du Fresnoy in 1753, followed another century later by Jules Quicherat, who beavered away to produce a five-volume work that

most accept as the definitive work on the Maid's life, trial and death. But on what foundations do these three works rely? One from the seventeenth century, a second from the eighteenth century and a final work from the nineteenth century hardly constitute an unbroken chain of observation and assessment leading back to the early fifteenth century.

There are more than a few misconceptions attached to the legend of her trial, which did not result from accusations of witchcraft raised against her by the French Inquisition, a precursor to the more infamous Spanish Inquisition. According to the aforementioned Notre Dame documents, the only representative of that body present at the trial was Jean LeMaître who, ignoring threats from the English contingent, kept raising objections over the illegality and shambolic ineptitude of the proceedings. The Maid was tried for claiming that the voices she heard were of divine origin and for wearing male attire in contravention of the dictate expressed in the Bible, the Book of Deuteronomy 22:5, which forbade any kind of cross-dressing. There were allegedly other charges relating to her wearing armour and disporting herself at the head of an army but this too fails to ring true as women in armour leading fourteenth- and fifteenth-century armies were far more common than one might imagine today.

Jeanne de Montfort (d. 1374) organized the defence of Hennebont before, clad in armour and at the head of a 300-strong column of cavalry, she fought her way through to Brest. In 1346, Philippa of Hainault, wife of the English King Edward III, led an army against 12,000 Scottish invaders in her husband's absence; also in the fourteenth century, Jeanne de Belleville, the Lioness of Brittany, divided her time between preying on English shipping in the Channel and leading her army in northern France; and, in 1383, none other than Pope Boniface wrote in glowing terms of the deeds of Genoese ladies who, clad in their armour, fought in the Crusades. Margaret of Denmark, Jeanne de Penthièvre, Jacqueline of Bavaria, Isabella of Lorraine and Jeanne de Châtillon all wore armour and led armies in their time. Even the treacherous Burgundians, allied to the English invaders and so clamorous for the Maid's death, had female artillery squads. France was teeming with martial maidens in armour and if this failed to irk the Pope, why would the clerics of Rouen get so enraged over one more example?

More suspicions are raised by the alleged trial records, which depict the defendant as a highly articulate and well-read person who engaged in such stunningly erudite banter with her prosecutors and demonstrated such a grasp of the finer points of theology that she drew grudging admiration even from those determined she would burn. At the time of her alleged trial, she would have been just nineteen and still illiterate, so such impressive knowledge seems unlikely. It also seems clear that, if indeed the trial and execution happened, she did not, as legend would have it, stick to her guns until the bitter end. On the morning of 24 May 1431, she was taken out for execution and, faced with such a gruesome end, she opted to recant all in exchange for life imprisonment; she acknowledged that her 'voices' were not divine and promised to shun male attire in the future. Her abjuration was accepted but when the bishops paid her a surprise visit in prison on 29 May they again found her dressed as a man and immediately pronounced her a relapsed heretic who should burn at the stake the very next day. Tied to a stake in Rouen's Old Market on 30 May 1431, this is supposedly what happened.

To further cloud the issue, some maintain that the so-called Maid did not burn at Rouen because documents found in that city's archives purport the city officials to have authorized a payment of 210 livres to her 'for services rendered by her at the siege of the said city' on 1 August 1439. These highly suspect documents were first trotted out by the French politician François Daniel Polluche at the close of the eighteenth century and given credence the following century by the Belgian antiquarian Joseph Octave Delepierre. In 1898, Dr E. Cobham Brewer, he of *Brewer's Dictionary of Phrase and Fable* fame, wrote:

M. Octave Delepierre has published a pamphlet, called *Doute Historique*, to deny the tradition that Joan of Arc was burned at Rouen for sorcery. He cites a document discovered by Father Vignier in the seventeenth century, in the archives of Metz, to prove that she became the wife of Sieur des Armoise, with whom she resided at Metz, and became the mother of a family. Vignier subsequently found in the family muniment-chest the contract of marriage between Robert des Armoise, knight, and Jeanne D'Arcy, surnamed the Maid of Orleans. In 1740 there were found in the archives of the Maison de Ville d'Orléans records of several payments to certain messengers from Joan to her brother John, bearing the dates 1435, 1436. There is also the entry of a presentation from the council of the city to the Maid, for her services at the siege (dated 1439). M. Delepierre has brought forward a host of other documents to corroborate the same fact, and show that the tale of her martyrdom was invented to throw odium on the English.

There are other sources that claim Joan was alive after 1431. The ancient registers of the Maison de Ville, Orléans, and *The Chronicle of the Dean of St Thibault-de-Metz* both make reference to a post-Rouen Joan. Polluche laid out his arguments in *Problème Historique sur la Pucelle d'Orléans* (1749), forming in part the foundation for Delepierre, who first published his findings in the *Athenaeum* dated 15 September 1855. Either way, there seems to be a great deal of doubt as to the veracity of the tale of Jeanne d'Arc, with major question marks over every detail from her name and nationality right through to her exploits, trial and death.

◄○►

ELIZABETH BÁTHORY: THE REAL COUNTESS DRACULA

IT IS PROBABLY fair to say that no other woman in history has been as unjustly vilified as Elizabeth Báthory. More usually referred to today as Countess Dracula, she was believed by many to have bathed in the blood of virgins to retain her great beauty, and to have variously been a vampire or a werewolf. Between 1600 and 1610 the Hungarian allegedly murdered over 650 virgins from the seventeen villages surrounding her castle and under her feudal control which, given the population of early seventeenth-century rural Hungary, does seems a mite ambitious – the combined population of those seventeen villages numbered fewer than 400. As with the present reputation of Vlad Dracula, one-time ruler of Wallachia in modern Romania, all such tales are prurient fantasy.

It is interesting to note that the first mention of the abduction of those 650 virgins to provide the countess's unusual bathwater is not made until 1729 – over a century after her death. This same source was also responsible for conjuring up allegations of cannibalism, vampiric cavortings and the sado-sexual torture of as many girls again. The lot of underlings in any early seventeenth-century Hungarian household was not a happy one, with vicious beatings a common response to the slightest transgression and, in such brutality, Báthory was no different to her peers. Her ultimate downfall, however, was her wealth, and it seems likely that she was the victim of greed and political manoeuvring in the end. But who wanted her out of the way and why?

Born into great wealth and privilege in Nyírbátor, which stands in the extreme west of modern Hungary, at the age of ten Báthory was betrothed to sixteen-year-old Ferenc Nádasdy. A political marriage to form an alliance between the two most powerful families in the realm, this was no love-match and within a few years Ferenc was preoccupied with various wars, leaving Elizabeth to further her own education. By the time he died in 1604, at the age of forty-eight, Báthory had developed into a formidable woman who was not only fluent in several languages, including Latin and Greek, but also a lady of independent mind who was unwilling to 'know her place' in what was then a very male-dominated society. This was a time when few of the Hungarian nobility could even write their own name and Báthory was never one to baulk at ruffling a few feathers. As she was now in control of the combined Báthory–Nádasdy fortune, avaricious eyes were turning in her direction and the rumour mill was in full swing. All of Báthory's senior couriers and advisors were women, so malicious gossip that her court was nothing but a thinly disguised coven of witches was soon circulating. Something had to be done to put Báthory in her place.

The main players in this plot were King Matthias II of Hungary and his prime minister, György Thurzó, who was also Báthory's cousin. Perhaps unwisely, Báthory was constantly pestering the morally and financially bankrupt Matthias to pay his massive debts to the Báthory estates, while Thurzó himself owed her more than he could ever hope to repay. He had already tried to wipe that particular slate clean with a cynical proposal of marriage, only to have Báthory laugh in his face. Matthias ordered Thurzó to bring Báthory down but to tread carefully as she had many powerful allies throughout Hungary and nearby Poland, which was ruled by her uncle, King Stephen Báthory. His plans laid, Thurzó arrested Báthory on 29 December 1609 or 1610 (the sources vary), claiming to have caught her quite literally red-handed, in the middle of torturing one poor girl as another victim lay dead to one side. This is what Thurzó told everyone, but his warrant, which detailed no charges at all, was raised after the arrest and no one ever had the chance to interview the surviving girl or view the body of the deceased. It seems Thurzó made it all up for dramatic effect.

Keeping her under house arrest, Thurzó dragged away four of her closest and most trusted members of staff – Ilona-Jó, Dóra, Kata and János Ficzkó – to be tortured until they agreed to corroborate everything he alleged. Having been deprived of assorted body parts and subjected to Thurzó's fire pit, all four agreed that Báthory was indeed a witch who practised the dark arts in her castle, and that she routinely tortured and murdered virgin girls on her satanic altar. With one of his closest friends as the appointed judge, Thurzó also stacked the jury box with friends and dependants, going to trial on 2 January 1611, but he made such a hash of things that he was forced to call a halt to his own calamitous proceedings.

By the start of the second trial on 7 January, Thurzó had miraculously found what he claimed to be Báthory's own lurid record of all her satanic and murderous deeds. But the handwriting quite obviously bore no resemblance to the known examples of her hand on other contemporary documents. To sidestep the possibility of any further awkward questioning of his 'evidence', Thurzó ordered that the trial should continue in Latin with some of the witnesses being led into the court bound and gagged so they could only nod or shake their heads to the questions put to them. Witnesses who were allowed to talk delivered nothing but hearsay 'evidence'. While glaring untruths were allowed into evidence by the judge, despite known

THE LURID LEGEND

Regardless of the fact that her alleged crimes were the invention of men after her money, the mythical Elizabeth Báthory has spawned a veritable industry of books, plays, films, and even toys and video games.

The Brothers Grimm featured her as a demonic spectre in some of their darker tales and she also inspired the first ever lesbian vampire novel, *Carmilla* (1871) by Sheridan Le Fanu, which went on to inspire *Dracula* by Bram Stoker. She was also the inspiration for Leopold von Sacher-Masoch – the man who gave his name to masochism – to pen his famous novella *Eternal Youth* (1874).

In all, the lurid legend of Báthory has inspired or featured in fifty-eight novels, four poems and twelve plays to date, as well as countless TV programmes – the latest being *American Horror Story: Hotel* (2015) with Lady Gaga playing the Báthory-based Countess – forty-seven feature films, eighteen operas and musicals, and thirty-four heavy-metal songs. She is also, rather disturbingly, a bestseller in the 'Living Dead Dolls' range, outselling both Dracula and Jack the Ripper.

chronology refuting them, anything inconvenient to a guilty verdict was ruled inadmissible. Not one member of the families of Báthory's alleged victims was called and the scribes documenting the proceedings had to sit up half the night rewriting their own transcripts to iron out any irksome inconsistencies and contradictions. Thurzó's circus was a risible farce with Báthory herself having the good sense neither to enter a plea nor attend the charade.

Naturally, with the dice loaded, Thurzó and Matthias had their way and, as Báthory was being pronounced guilty on all charges, Thurzó's wife was steaming through Báthory's castle harvesting anything of value that took her fancy. With the debts of Matthias and Thurzó declared null and void, the bulk of Báthory's lands and wealth was divided up between the interested parties as the four core witnesses were taken out for immediate execution, just to keep things neat and tidy. Knowing he had gone as far as he dared, Thurzó did not have Báthory walled up in a chamber to starve to death, as legend would have us believe, but allowed her to remain at her castle at Čachtice in the Carpathian Mountains providing she kept her mouth shut and didn't make waves. There she remained, dying of natural causes in 1614 at the age of fifty-four.

But, no matter how outlandish the charges laid against her by Thurzó, there was no mention of any gory bathing habits and certainly no mention of blood-guzzling vampiric ritual; even Thurzó was not that imaginative. Instead this was born of the highly colourful mind of a decidedly unbalanced Jesuit called László Turóczi in his book

Ungaria Suis cum Regibus Compendio Data, or *A Short Description of Hungary together with its Kings* (1729). Determined to make his tome a bit of a page-turner, Turóczi seemingly invented all the blood-bathing and satanic practice. If ever proof was required of the adage that a good lie can travel halfway round the world before truth gets its boots on, then this is it.

——◇——

DOCTOR JAMES BARRY:
A NECESSARY DISGUISE

ALTHOUGH THE NOTION of a female Pope has no foundation (see page 35), some women have mounted spectacular cross-dressing frauds of considerable endurance, and none more so than the girl who rose to high rank in the nineteenth-century British Army.

With her name, date of birth and parentage still debated to this day, the girl who was to become Dr James Barry was born in Cork, perhaps in 1789 or 1792, and raised in the London-based artistic commune presided over by the influential Irish artist James Barry. Also in that group was Mary Ann Bulkley, the artist's sister, referred to by the young Barry as her aunt although some suspect she was in fact her mother. Also in the coterie were the exiled Venezuelan revolutionary General Francisco de Miranda and David Steuart Erskine, the 11th Earl of Buchan. Peripheral to the group were more stable and powerful figures such as Fitzroy Somerset, better known as Lord Raglan, and his brother, Lord Charles Somerset, later Governor of the Cape Colony in South Africa. In short, the girl, then going by the name of Margaret, was raised with some extremely well-connected strings to pull in later life.

At some later point she abandoned the use of Margaret, choosing instead to be known as Miranda after the general who, along with Erskine, a dedicated if slightly eccentric proponent of women's rights to education, strongly advised his namesake that if she really wanted to study medicine, as was her avowed intention, then she would only succeed if she adopted a male persona. At the time this ruse was mooted, it would be another fifty-odd years before women were allowed to study and practise medicine: the UK's first openly female doctor, Elizabeth Garrett, qualified in 1865. Either way, whether the 'game' started as a joke or as some misguided sociological experiment by Erskine, this now set the pattern for Miranda's life. Cram-tutored by Dr Edward Fryer, who had attended the artist James Barry in his last and fatal illness, Miranda soaked up medical knowledge at such an alarming rate that, under the name of James Miranda Steuart Barry, she entered the Medical School of Edinburgh University in November 1809. Short of stature, slight of build and delicate of features, some in the faculty smelled a rat – but the wrong rat. They thought the sylph-like Barry to be but a boy and thus too young to take the final exams in 1812. But Erskine, claiming to know for sure that Barry was of age, browbeat the faculty into relenting. Barry sat her finals to pass out top of class with a thesis on femoral hernias which, dedicated to Erskine, she wrote entirely in Latin, just to prove her point.

Returning to London for further training at Guy's and St Thomas', Barry, still in her late teens or early twenties, was admitted to the Royal College of Surgeons in 1813 before joining the Army Medical Department, where she proved extremely able but also extremely unpopular. Foulmouthed and given to a candour bordering on callous indifference, Barry felt no restraint in criticizing others for their error or inefficiency – whatever their rank – but those upon whom she unleashed her spleen felt they had no choice but to endure such humiliations because of the influence Barry so obviously wielded throughout Whitehall in particular and London in general. In 1816, by which time Barry held the rank of Lieutenant-Surgeon, she was posted to Cape Town in South Africa for attachment to the Table Bay Military Hospital as an assistant surgeon. Wasting no time on pleasantries, on arrival she immediately informed her senior officer, Surgeon-Major McNab, that she would not be needing the meagre quarters assigned her as she would be staying at the Governor's residence.

Over the following decade, Barry and the Governor, Lord Charles Somerset, grew close, so close in fact that Cape Town gossip was soon buzzing with speculation of a homosexual affair. And that gossip kicked into overdrive after Somerset appointed the junior Barry to the position of Inspector General of all medical facilities in the province. Perhaps their relationship did extend to the physical; upon her death Barry was discovered to have stretch marks and, in 1819, she suddenly quit Cape Town for Britain and went into hiding for several months, both suggestive of pregnancy. She also went AWOL in 1829 to return to England to tend to the stricken Lord Charles Somerset, who had quit the governorship in 1826 due to ill health.

These were not her only bouts of absenteeism, any one of which would have seen another officer facing court martial. Yet not once was Barry so much as questioned over her abandonments of post.

Her high-handed approach to military life aside, her work in South Africa was exemplary. Years ahead of her time, she instituted stringent hygiene regimes in all military hospitals as well as a healthcare plan for the families of all serving soldiers. On 25 July 1826, in a rushed operation on

CLASHES WITH FLORENCE NIGHTINGALE

In 1854, during the Crimean War, Dr Barry instituted her stringent hygiene regimes to such an extent that the wounded treated in facilities under her direct control enjoyed the highest survival rates of the war. Her advanced thinking on how a hospital should be run caused repeated and hostile clashes with Florence Nightingale. Nightingale was an adherent of the Miasma theory, holding that all diseases and infections were caused by foul vapours; she would later lampoon Louis Pasteur for his suggestion that disease was caused by germs. Barry and Nightingale, whose unit had one of the highest death rates in the Crimea, frequently came to loggerheads with the latter describing 'him' as 'the most brutish person I have ever met'.

a kitchen table, she performed the first documented successful Caesarean section by a European, on Wilhelmina Munnik, the wife of Thomas Munnik, a local merchant. This was one of the first such procedures in which both mother and child survived, and the grateful couple named the child James Barry Munnik. That boy's descendant, James Barry Munnik Hertzog, would later serve as Prime Minister of South Africa between 1924–39. As to Barry's personal life, this was at best contradictory. She was always extremely popular with the ladies who found 'him' easy to talk to; no surprise there! She was also an outrageous flirt and once had to fight a pistol duel with Captain Josias Cloete, aide-de-camp to the Governor, after being over-familiar with the Captain's lady friend. Both survived to become the best of friends.

After a brief tour of duty in Canada, and having reached the rank of Inspector General of Military Hospitals, the equivalent of Brigadier General, Barry was invalided back to London where, on 25 July 1865, she died. She had left explicit instructions that she was to be buried immediately in the clothes in which she expired but a charwoman, Sophia Bishop, decided to ignore this and lay her out properly. She had already seen more than enough by the time Surgeon-Major D. R. McKinnon arrived to bundle her out of the room before issuing a death certificate stating Barry to have been a male deceased of dysentery. Hot on McKinnon's heels came a squad of the Victorian era's equivalent of the Special Branch, who arrived in unmarked carriages to remove every last scrap of paper from Barry's Marylebone home, and most of her personal items. Barry's Jamaican manservant, John, was cautioned in the strongest possible terms to forget anything he had heard or seen before being handed an envelope of money and a one-way ticket home, and being taken straight to the docks in one of the carriages. Held under virtual arrest in his cabin by three black-clad Victorian heavies until his ship was due to depart, he was never heard from again.

A few days later, Sophia Bishop visited McKinnon to demand payment for her own silence and, when he threw her out on her ear, she went straight to the newspapers to tell her story. But by this time Barry had been buried with full military honours in London's Kensal Green Cemetery and all her records mysteriously disappeared from the War Office; it was as if the good Doctor Barry never existed. As one might imagine, there has been much lurid speculation as to the real identity of James Miranda Steuart Barry; was she the product of some illicit royal dalliance? She certainly had some seriously powerful people watching over her life.

———◦———

PHANTOMS AND FACE PAINT: THE WESTERN MYTH OF THE BLACK-CLAD NINJA

MUCH OF WHAT many of us think we know about the cultural history of Japan is pretty wide of the mark. For example, sushi is not raw fish, but actually any dish based on vinegared rice – which may or not contain sashimi, which *is* raw fish (or occasionally meat), thinly sliced; sake is not rice wine but rather a brewed product and thus more akin to a strong beer. And no one in Japan had even heard of a ninja until the term was invented and misapplied by Europeans.

'Japan' itself is in fact an exonym of Chinese origin and only grudgingly adopted by certain sectors of Japanese commerce anxious to grease the wheels of tourism. Since ancient times, to the indigenous population the country has been Nippon or Nihon, which are the two accepted and alternative readings of the same pictogram indicating 'the birthplace of the sun'. Of the two, the former is more popular with the older generation and the latter more so with Japanese youth. 'Japan' would be understood by most to mean some kind of bread. In those same ancient times the much larger China referred to Nippon as *Wa*, meaning small and obedient, but the diplomatic ripples caused by this condescending terminology eventually forced the Chinese to abandon this in favour of *Jihpun*, their own term for sunrise, which also produced the more poetic Land of the Rising Sun. These were the two names picked up by Westerners trading with China to whom Japan was still a closed door.

After the Second World War, a veritable tsunami of Western culture washed over Nippon, and everything from train seats to the height of kitchen counters had to be remodelled as the national average height shot up due to increased protein consumption driven by Western-style diets. According to the Japanese Ministry of Education, by the age of eleven the average child is now a staggering six inches taller than fifty years ago. But, despite the invasion by cola, burgers and fries, there are still many historical aspects of Nipponese life that remain grossly misunderstood by Westerners.

Western cinematic audiences have an insatiable appetite for films depicting the gymnastic antics of nimble ninjas who, after leaping fifteen feet in the air, descend to kill a dozen or so adversaries with nothing but their bare hands and a broken chopstick. So it may come as a surprise to many that the typical so-called ninja was usually female, middle-aged and spent most of her time in domestic service. So how did we end up with the notion of the lethal assassin creeping about in black pyjamas?

'Ninja' made its first appearance in print in English when it was used by Ian Fleming in his novel *You Only Live Twice* (1964). Its subsequent usage was so limited that it was denied admittance to the twenty-volume *Oxford English Dictionary: Second Edition* (1989). The word was an invention of the English-speaking West of the nineteenth century that, finding the Japanese *shinobi no mono* – a person of stealth – too cumbersome, resorted to the much older on'yomi, or Sino–Japanese equivalents of 'nin' (stealth) and 'ja' (person). First noted in Japan as early as the eighth century, *shinobi* denoted a servant in a house of particular interest – cook, gardener, maid, concubine, or whatever – who was willing to sell intelligence as to the day-to-day comings and goings of visitors and overheard conversations. The *shinobi* were never expected or trusted to handle any 'wet work' – if the *shinobi*'s handlers thought it was time to terminate their employer then a rogue samurai or some other such person was brought in to handle any killing. So, Japan certainly had its own coterie of killers-for-hire but they went by various other names meaning assassin or the more flowery 'walker in the shadows' – never *shinobi* and certainly not the Western-invented *ninja*.

The notion of the black-clad killer arose from the stage conventions of the traditional style of kabuki theatre in which the actors do not leave the stage during scene changes. Then, as now, the stagehands simply walked about the stage to effect whatever changes were required, but always dressed in black to indicate to the audience that they were not part of the story. By extension, should the storyline call for a killer to infiltrate the action but remain unseen to the other players, then he too would move about the stage dressed in black to indicate his 'invisibility' to the audience. Unfortunately, this left Western viewers of kabuki plays with the notion that hired killers in Japan always crept about in black.

That said, the Western appetite for the ninja myth gave birth to the present genre of martial arts films which, in turn, have convinced some viewers that the Japanese are somehow anatomically superior to everyone else on the planet. But no one in Japan can run up the sides of buildings or walk on water. The brick-breaking and head-butting of blocks in some martial arts involves much careful preparation. Obviously, as ninjas never existed under that name, all the 'genuine replicas' of ninja weapons advertised on the internet are, like the mace-and-chain allegedly swung with murderous intent by English knights, modern inventions. While there are indeed countless historical references to the use of *shuriken* (hand-hidden blades) by killers and thugs, these seem to have been nothing more sophisticated than sharpened spikes or double-ended blades. Despite what you see in the movies, no one, be they European or Japanese, can throw a knife with sufficient force to embed itself in the chest of some baddie, so *shuriken* were only thrown in the hope of persuading a pursuer to abandon the chase. Either way, the 'death star' *shuriken* is itself likely a modern invention. In fact, the assassins of early Japan were not traditionalists; as soon as firearms and explosives became available, they became the weapons of choice. With the completion of the contract being the overriding objective, bombs and guns were favoured over traditional weapons from the mid-1500s onwards.

The samurai, of course, were a different matter. While they certainly did exist, they were hardly the men of honour depicted in sword-and-sake epics today. As with the knights of Old England, who were basically thugs in tin suits, the samurai were a warrior elite who reserved honourable behaviour for those who could best appreciate it – themselves. No courtesy or act of chivalry was squandered on the lower orders as the samurai went about the bidding of his paymaster without question. Much of the bidding was also pretty underhand, dishonourable and treacherous. All the fanciful notions about some imagined code of practice called *bushido*, or the way of the warrior, were largely the invention of Japanese writer and diplomat Nitobe Inazo for his *Bushido: The Soul of Japan* (1899). Although *bushido* as a term made a handful of appearances in pre-twentieth-century Japanese literature, other terms such as *mononofu*, *tsuwamono* or *saburau* were more common. If dishonoured, a samurai might be expected to commit *seppuku*, the form of ritualistic suicide erroneously called *hara-kiri* by Westerners, but which was rarely the gruesome spectacle of popular imagination. Often, the samurai picking up a knife was taken as indication of suicidal intent, and then the victim's 'best man' was given the nod to cut off his friend's head.

No matter how frequently it is stated, the fact is that karate did not evolve in feudal Japan to enable the peasants

NIGHTINGALE NO FUN

The traditional white face mask of the geisha used to be achieved with lead-based cosmetics, but when the dangers of such applications became apparent it was replaced by preparations based on powdered rice. Because both made the teeth look an unhealthy yellow in contrast, geisha used to paint them black.

Removal of the white mask was achieved with *uguisu no fun*, or nightingale faeces. Arthur Golden's 1997 novel, *Memoirs of a Geisha*, made into a film by Steven Spielberg in 2005, made the purity and use of *uguisu no fun* so pivotal to one particular aspect of the plot that, after seeing the film, some were left with the erroneous impression that bird poo was an ancient Japanese beauty treatment. Since then, the rich and famous have been willing to pay up to $250 a time for a 'geisha facial' which involves their faces being smeared with nightingale 'no fun' – perhaps someone should tell them that the pigeons will happily 'anoint' them for free.

to punch through the bamboo armour of the oppressive samurai. Not only was samurai armour made of stiffened leather and metal plates, but karate was not a skill developed in early Japan. Chinese Shaolin monks of the

Tang Dynasty (AD 618–907) introduced such skills when visiting Okinawa, the principal island of the ancient and independent Ryukyu Kingdom, where it was for centuries known as 'China hand' or 'Tang hand'. In 1922 the Japanese Ministry of Education invited Okinawan martial-arts master Gichin Funakoshi to give a demonstration of his skills and Japan went China-hand-mad. But, due to the historic and ongoing hostilities with China, the Japanese decided to rename their new hobby *karate*, meaning 'empty hand', to obscure its Chinese origins.

And, just as everyone in the West has a mental image of a ninja or a samurai, the very mention of geisha conjures up images of white-faced and elaborately clad women who are essentially highly refined and highly paid sex workers. Not only is such a perception completely erroneous and regarded in Japan as ignorant and offensive, but all geisha were originally male – as indeed a few still are.

With their history dating back to the early thirteenth century, the true geisha has never been involved in the sex-for-sale industry. The name translates as a person skilled in the arts, and it takes about five years of unpaid study to attain such rank. Until the eighteenth century all geisha were men who were hired on an individual basis for a small group meeting in a teahouse to provide entertainment in the form of music, poetry or even bawdy tales of yore. Sometimes geisha were hired in groups to ensure larger private functions went well by mixing with the guests, making sure everyone felt welcome and important before putting on assorted entertainments. To suggest that any geisha, male or female, would sleep with the guests for payment is akin to expecting a famous operatic diva to offer the same services if hired to sing at a private and high-class function in the West.

The first woman recorded as joining the ranks of the geisha was Kikuya, an entertainer in the Fukagawa district of Tokyo. Already a proficient singer and musician, she quickly retrained as a geisha around 1750 and became so popular that many other women followed her lead. In Tokyo in 1770 the male geisha still outnumbered their female counterparts two to one, but by 1775 that ratio had shifted to an even split and, by 1800, the male geisha were outnumbered. This takeover continued until the 1920s when there were about 75,000 female geisha operating throughout Japan, with the number of males by then dwindled to fewer than a hundred nationwide. Today it is very different; the only 'geisha' the tourist will see is a poor reflection, kimonoed and white-faced in pale imitation to pose for holiday snaps, while the real thing is hidden away. The only way to visit a geisha house is by invitation. As the current cost of the five-year training can exceed £350,000 (which the *maiko*, or geisha-in-training, is expected to repay her sponsor once working), just to have a geisha sing you a couple of songs in the guarded privacy of a formal teahouse will cost something approaching £1,500.

POPE JOAN: A WOMAN ON THE FISHERMAN'S THRONE

To ENDURING VATICAN chagrin, belief in the existence of a ninth-century female Pope, Joan, refuses to die, with books and films focusing on her alleged reign still being turned out. Although early accounts vary, the standard version of the story alleges that, after the death of Pope Leo IV (17 July 855), a woman masquerading as the Englishman John Anglicus hoodwinked the Vatican cardinals into electing her to the papal throne from which she reigned for some two and a half years before her true gender was discovered in a very public and dramatic manner. Although an inspection of the chronology swiftly demolishes most if not all of her alleged history, we are still left with the mystery surrounding who started the tale in the first place and to what end.

First mention of the scandal is noted in the eleventh-century writings of Marianus Scotus of the Abbey of St Martin, Cologne, which assert (and note the author's mistaken date): 'In AD 854 Joanna, a woman, succeeded [Pope] Leo [IV] and reigned for two years, five months and four days.' Next to throw his hat into this ring was the twelfth-century scribe Sigebert de Gembloux, who alleged: 'It is reported that this John was a female and that she conceived a child by one of her servants.' But the most famous and detailed of all such early mentions is found in *The Chronicle of the Popes and Emperors* by Martin of Poland (d. 1278), a bishop-chronicler who maintained: 'After Leo, John Anglicus, a native of Mainz [a city in Germany's Rhineland, although others have her a native of Metz in north-eastern France], reigned two years five months and four days. It is claimed that this John was a woman who, when a girl, had been brought to Athens in the clothes of a man by a certain lover.'

Once in that city, according to Martin, she excelled in science and philosophy until she had no equal; she next moved to Rome where she maintained her deception to teach many of the great minds of the day, with her reputation

for virtue and knowledge growing to such pitch that she was a natural choice for Pope. Martin further states, 'While Pope she became pregnant and through ignorance of the exact time of the birth she was delivered of a child while in procession from St Peter's to the Lateran, in a narrow lane between the Colosseum and St Clement's Church, in the street.' At this point, most accounts agree that both mother and child were beaten to death by the indignant mob. 'The Lord Pope always turns aside from this street [in procession] and it is believed by many that this is done for abhorrence of the event.'

It is important to bear in mind that medieval scribes and chroniclers were the photocopiers of their day, diligently replicating each other's work while inserting additions to cater to the prejudices of whoever was paying for the finished product. Once a genuine error or a malicious spoof got into the mix, it was destined for centuries of meticulous repetition. It was also common for those with a particular axe to grind in later centuries to bolster their fraud by the insertion of supportive additions into much earlier works – and it is significant that, in some hand-scribed copies of Martin's book, the lover who took Joan to Athens is referred to as her 'sweetheart' – a term not known before 1290 – and reference to her being pregnant presents her as being 'in the family way', an expression not known prior to the mid-seventeenth century.

Then there is the chronology of the papal line itself; the longest gap between any two Popes did indeed occur in 855, the year of Joan's alleged ascension, after Leo IV died to leave in his wake a most undignified squabble over the succession. First choice was Hadrian, Cardinal of St Marco, but he had the good sense to turn the job down flat. Second choice was Benedict, whose rule was immediately interrupted by a group of militant bishops who carted him off to prison to make way for their choice of Anastasius, a machinating back-stabber who had been anathematized and exiled by Leo IV. But, when he and his supporters realized their coup was stillborn, Benedict was hurriedly released, dusted down and reinstated as if nothing had happened. This game of musical thrones ran from 17 July 855 until 29 September the same year to give us Leo IV (847–55), followed by Benedict III (855–8) and Nicholas I (858–67), all of which leaves no room for a papal reign spanning any two years of the decade commencing in 850. Nor is there a single contemporary historical reference to any Pope John/Joan in that decade or to the violent nature of her death in the streets at the hands of a mob.

Despite this mountain of evidence to the contrary, those who still cling to their belief in a female Pope love to point out that papal processions, which once went down the narrow street mentioned by Martin of Poland, have avoided it for centuries. Pro-Joanists love to point out that this street, one of a tiny enclave of similar streets between the Colosseum and St Clement's Church, is called Vicus Papessa, but this should not be translated as the 'Street of the Female Pope'. The street was not called that until the tenth century, when it was renamed in honour of the wife of Giovanni Pape, a rich merchant who lived there, so the name properly translates as the altogether less intriguing Mrs Pape Street. Short of traipsing round in circles all day, papal processions would honour certain streets adjacent to their route with inclusion, providing the residents decked out the thoroughfare in a suitable manner and put a healthy sum into the Vatican coffers for the privilege. Apparently, Mrs Pape loved the pomp and ceremony of papal processions so Mr Pape indulged her but, when the Pape family died out, the Vatican no longer had any incentive to venture down the steep and narrow street.

There is also the matter of an admittedly puzzling throne-like marble chair held in the Vatican Museum; once one of a pair – Napoleon is thought to have looted the other – this has a large keyhole shape cut out of the seat. This has been eagerly seized upon by pro-Joanists, who maintain that both chairs were made in the post-Joan era to ensure that no woman could ever again perpetrate such a fraud. According to that lobby, once the papal candidate had been selected, he was required to sit on one such chair with his genitalia visible to the voters assembled in a special viewing chamber on the floor below. Next, the cleric selected to remain in the upper chamber with the candidate was required to reach under the chair and, taking hold of said papal appendage, pronounce, 'Testiculos habet et bene pendentes', or 'He has testicles and they hang well', this no doubt affording great comfort to all concerned. Needless to say, no such 'ceremony' has ever been enacted. Some say these chairs were simply commodes but the fact that the uprights are raked back at 45 degrees makes this unlikely. Others maintain that they were birthing-chairs. Either way, they long pre-date the alleged time of Pope Joan and, indeed, the advent of the Vatican itself. Which brings us back to the core question: who started the silly story and why did they do it?

ON THE BIG SCREEN

The Vatican's distaste for the notion of a woman once having hoodwinked the cardinals into appointing her Pope has not been made any better by the constant parade of books, plays and films promoting the idea as fact.

The most recent venture into celluloid was *Pope Joan* (2009), a German film with Johanna Wokalek in the title role, which attracted disdain from the Vatican for billing itself as a 'true story'. *L'Avvenire*, the Catholic newspaper, branded the film a vacuous hoax and an enterprise of little vision but this did not stop it achieving box office success and placing it in the Italian Top Ten Movie List for 2009/2010, taking second position just behind *Sex and the City 2*.

At the beginning of the sixteenth century there was growing dissatisfaction across Europe over the way the Vatican conducted itself – especially when it came to the selling of indulgences. These were dispensations for sins, available only to the rich, who could thus skip their allotted time of penance in Purgatory and go straight to Heaven. When indulgences were made available to cover sins not yet committed – I'll have two murders and one rape, to go, please – it was this coffer-filling scam run by the Vatican which, more than anything else, led to the foundation of the Protestant reform movement and, soon after, the Protestant Church itself. Determined to make its mark, this new movement did everything it could to blacken the name of the opposition in Rome. Its adherents' first successful propaganda coup was the spreading of gruesome tales about the activities of the Spanish Inquisition, which was nowhere near as draconian or punitive as the Protestant machine painted it, and then they came up with the idea of promoting the ultimate anathema to the Vatican – a female Pope.

Historian Edward Gibbon, author of *The History of the Decline and Fall of the Roman Empire* (1776), argued that the inspiration for this notion might well have been the Vatican scandal known as the Pornocracy or the Rule of Harlots. This began with the ascension of Pope Sergius III in 904, a time conveniently close to the alleged time of Pope Joan. A weak and vacillating man, Sergius immediately fell under the spell of Theodora, the beautiful but viper-like wife of Rome's leading Consul,

Theophylact, Count of Tusculum, and a woman who used her sexual charms to keep Sergius and others in the Vatican compliant to her ambitions. Soon tiring of being so hands-on with Sergius, Theodora passed that duty to her fifteen-year-old daughter, Marozia. Despite her youth, Marozia immediately raised the stakes and, by engineering many political murders in the Vatican, made the Borgias look like amateurs.

Her illegitimate son by Sergius would become Pope John XI (931–5), and two of her grandsons, two of her great-grandsons and one great-great-grandson each took their turn on the Chair of St Peter – a unique achievement in the history of the Vatican. Marozia bore the title of Senatrix and Patricia of Rome – the female equivalent of Senator and Patrician – bestowed on her by Pope John X (914–28), yet another of her mother's lovers. She died in 937, after which the Pornocracy pretty much fizzled out.

The Protestant propagandists reasoned that if a woman had indeed been the real power behind the papal throne, they could 'rebrand' this scandal in the form of an actual female Pope. That just left them with the need to generate some suitable early references to the lady. Remember the strange appearance of 'sweetheart' and 'in the family way' found in copies of Martin of Poland's work? It should also be said that in some of the earliest known copies of his *Chronicle of the Popes and Emperors*, those kept safe from meddling hands, no mention of Pope Joan can be found. Also, many of the other references to Joan in other early works appear as footnotes or margin notes that are in a hand quite unlike that of the main text. So, if we accept Gibbon's suggestion that the sixteenth- and seventeenth-century Protestant propaganda machine simply resurrected the Pornocracy in the form of Pope Joan and concocted back-washed forgeries into medieval manuscripts, then all makes sense.

————◄O►————

TOKYO ROSE: THE WOMAN
WHO NEVER WAS

STILL REFERRED TO in popular culture today, the spectre of the non-existent Tokyo Rose continues to conjure up notions of a honey-voiced Japanese seductress who, throughout the Second World War, made daily radio broadcasts to taunt the American troops fighting the Japanese Army and Navy in the Pacific. These American troops claimed to have endured her cajoling taunts of their impending defeat and deaths while their loved ones betrayed them in the marriage beds at home, so it will come as a surprise to many that the mysterious Tokyo Rose never existed. That said, someone had to be framed as Tokyo Rose to save the postwar American administration from the political suicide of publicly branding their returning heroes a bunch of deluded hysterics. The patsy forced into President Truman's frame was the diminutive Iva Toguri, arrested and imprisoned for having been the woman who never was.

Born on 4 July 1916 to Japanese parents in Los Angeles, all-American Iva was a devout baseball fan and graduated from the University of California with a degree in zoology. In July 1941 she travelled to Japan to nurse a sick and dying aunt only to be caught left-footed by the Japanese bombing of Pearl Harbor, which brought the United States into the Second World War. While her parents were being interned as hostile aliens back home, Iva was enduring similar treatment in Japan for her refusal to renounce her American citizenship. She was eventually released from detention and found work as a typist at Tokyo Radio, where she met and married Filipe D'Aquino. The station put out propaganda programmes, in particular a daily show called *The Zero Hour*, which was hosted by an Australian POW called Major Charles Cousens who had been a radio personality in Sydney before the war. He had been removed from his prison camp by Major Shigetsugu Tsuneishi of the Psychological Warfare Division and told that if he did not comply he and ten other prisoners, selected at random, would be shot.

Deciding to do all he could to sabotage the venture, Cousens was teamed up with US Army Captain Wallace Ince and Lieutenant Norman Reyes. Once at Tokyo Radio, Cousens realized that Iva was a kindred spirit and 'recruited' her into the programme by convincing his Japanese handlers that her familiarity with colloquial American would prove an invaluable asset. Iva's input consisted of nothing more than doing a few links and introducing records from the musical selection, which she did under the name of Orphan Annie. Using a combination of voice tone, subtle innuendo and slang, the four did everything they could to ensure American listeners would be falling about laughing. Iva frequently addressed her audience as 'my fellow orphans' and even took the risky option of reminding the audience that they were listening to propaganda whenever the monitor stepped out of the studio. She also spent much of her meagre wages on basic medicines, which she passed under the table to Cousens to take back to camp. Had she been caught out in any such tricks she would, in all likelihood, have been shot.

After the capitulation of Japan in 1945, General MacArthur landed at Atsugi Airfield, some 20 miles from Yokohama, bringing with him a pack of rapacious journalists, each determined to interview General Tojo and track down the ghost that was Tokyo Rose. Two of the leading lights of this entourage were Clark Lee of the International News Service and Harry Brundidge of *Cosmopolitan* magazine, the latter putting out word that he would pay $250 to anyone who could point him in the right direction and a further $2,000 to the lady herself for an exclusive interview. In the commercial wreck that was Japan in 1945, this kind of money meant the difference between survival and oblivion – to put those offers into perspective, Iva's pay at Tokyo Radio was the equivalent of $7 a month. Perhaps inevitably, one of Iva's colleagues at the station, Leslie Nakashima, sold her name to Brundidge.

Never having heard of Tokyo Rose and labouring under the delusion that her self-satire of her limited input to *The Zero Hour* had made her some sort of heroine to the American forces, Iva, also delirious at the prospect of being paid today's equivalent of $50,000 for a single interview, eagerly agreed with Brundidge that she was indeed Tokyo

Rose and ready to talk. But to Brundidge's increasing alarm, Iva sat rocking with laughter at any suggestion of her having been some sort of honey-voiced femme fatale and reacted quite violently to any suggestion that she had ever broadcast anything to the detriment of the United States or its forces. All she wanted to talk about were the ploys she and Cousens had used to let listeners know that all had been tongue-in-cheek.

Next, hurled into a panic by his editors' refusal to be bound by the contract he had so obviously signed with a nobody, which left him liable for the $2,000, Brundidge took all his tapes and notes to General Elliott Thorpe, commander of the US Intelligence Corps in Japan, and urged him to arrest Iva as the traitor Tokyo Rose. And, just in case Thorpe failed to act, Brundridge also arranged for the gullible Iva to give a mass interview to over 300 reporters to place her in breach of the exclusivity clause of their contract and so render it void. The unwitting Iva gave her interview at the Yokohama Bund Hotel on 5 September 1945 with all present puzzled at her obviously revelling in what she misperceived as her newfound celebrity. The woman before them obviously had no idea who or what Tokyo Rose was believed to be.

Back in America, the right-wing media personality Walter Winchell, a mean-spirited but popular figure who seemingly took delight in using his media muscle to crush careers, latched onto the story, making demands on television and radio for Washington to have Iva arrested for treason and brought back to the States in chains. In Tokyo, the carrot-and-stick tactics of bribes and threats were brought to bear on Kenkichi Oki and George Mitsushio, two US-born employees at Tokyo Radio who had been in management positions above Iva. They were relentlessly groomed during the weeks preceding Iva's trial to get them 'word perfect' in their spoon-fed perjury. These two would testify at her trial – which began on 5 July 1949 – that she routinely made treasonable statements over the air and frequently mentioned specific American units and their location. When later admitting their testimony to have been a pack of lies, the two said in their defence that as they, unlike Iva, had renounced their American citizenship, they were condemned to remain in Japan under American occupational control, and that it had been made blisteringly clear to them just how unpleasant life could be made for them and their families if they did not do as ordered.

AXIS SALLY

Born in Portland, Maine, Mildred Gillars was the real American traitor-at-the-mic who broadcast from Berlin throughout the Second World War as Axis Sally, frequently signing off with a sneer at President Roosevelt and all his 'Jewish boyfriends'.

It was Gillars who goaded American servicemen about their impending defeat. She also made routine visits to POW camps to record demoralizing 'interviews' which, conducted under the muzzle of a gun, she would use in her show, *Home Sweet Home*.

Hunted through the ruins of post-war Germany, Gillars was finally returned to the United States where, on 10 March 1949, she was given a ten to thirty year prison sentence and a $10,000 fine. She first became eligible for parole in 1959 but, reluctant to face the public, she refused to apply and, in 1961, the Alderson Reformatory in West Virginia had to virtually throw her out onto the street to be rid of her.

Having 'found God', Gillars went to live at the Our Lady of Bethlehem Convent in Columbus, Ohio, where she taught German until she died in 1988.

Even the judge, carefully selected after a quiet word from Washington, would also later confess to have been operating under a politically dictated agendum resulting in Iva's trial being an utter disgrace. US District Judge Michael Roche acknowledged that he had consistently ruled out any evidence 'likely to confuse the jury as to her guilt' and to have then browbeaten that same jury into returning a guilty verdict on the last remaining charge after they had driven him to distraction by returning not-guilty verdicts on the other seven vaguely worded charges. Among the evidence disallowed by Roche was that of Cousens who, cleared of any wrongdoing on his return to Australia, where all had a good laugh at what he and Iva got away with on air, had travelled to the States at his own expense to testify that all she had ever done was a few links and interject sarcastic comments. Also disallowed were the repeated attempts by the defence to introduce into evidence that as early as August 1945 the US Office of War Information had published in the *New York Times* a report stating: 'There is no Tokyo Rose; the name is strictly a GI invention. Government monitors listening in twenty-four hours a day have never heard the words "Tokyo Rose" over any Japanese-controlled Far Eastern Radio.'

It would also doubtless have confused the jury to hear that General Theron L. Caudle, Assistant Attorney General of the US Army, had reported to the Attorney General's Office:

Considerable investigations have been conducted into this case and it appears that the identification of

Toguri as 'Tokyo Rose' is erroneous as her activity consisted of nothing more than the announcement of music selections. A few cylinders of her broadcasts and a large number of her scripts have been located and they, as well as the transcripts of the broadcasts of her program which were monitored by the Federal Communications Commission, do not disclose that she did anything more than introduce musical records. It is my opinion that Toguri's activities, particularly in view of the innocent nature of her broadcasts, are not sufficient to warrant her prosecution for treason.

Even six months before her arrest, the Eighth Army Legal Services was reporting: 'There is no evidence that she ever broadcast greetings to units by name or location or predicted military movements or attacks indicating that she had access to secret military information and plans as the Tokyo Rose of rumour and legend is reported to have done.'

But none of this could save Iva from the determination of the Truman administration to give the people what they wanted; the few who did speak out in her defence lived to regret it as she was thrown to the wolves with a sentence of ten years and a $10,000 fine. Paradoxically, while American bile was focused on the wholly innocent but supposedly 'foreign' Iva, the real American traitor-broadcaster Mildred Gillars was quietly being locked away. Broadcasting from Berlin as Axis Sally, it was this middle-class white woman from Maine who had taunted

American troops with tales of defeat and spousal infidelities, and all done in a sultry and seductive voice trained in minor acting roles in pre-war America.

After doing her time, Iva was released to settle in Chicago, receiving in 1977 a belated but nevertheless welcome full pardon from President Ford. Shortly before her death in 2006 she was also presented with the Edward J. Herlihy Citizenship Award by the American World War II Veterans Committee, which praised her for her stoical silence throughout her unjustly imposed ordeal, during which she never uttered a single cross word against her country.

————◁◦▷————

ROBIN HOOD:
FACT OR FOLKLORE?

ROBIN HOOD IS without doubt one of the most iconic figures of British popular culture, but the man at the heart of the legend (if, indeed, there is one and we are not looking at some composite figure or one of pure fiction) is impossible to nail down. The popular image of Robin has him as a loyal contemporary of King Richard I (reigned 1189–99), who, so keen to meet such a loyal if raffish subject, disguised himself as a merchant and rode through Sherwood as 'bait' to draw Robin out. But as the French-bred Richard couldn't speak a word of English and only spent a scant five months in England throughout his entire reign, a meeting of any kind would have been unlikely. Besides, the very first mention of Robin Hood the outlaw arises in *Piers Plowman*, an allegorical narrative penned by William Langland in the late 1370s, and the bulk of the Robin Hood ballads, first committed to parchment in the 1450s, mention a king called 'Edward' but give no indication as to his regnal number.

In keeping with the general public's deep-seated admiration for criminals of a certain type – Jessie James, Billy the Kid, Dick Turpin – people like to perceive Robin as the man who only robbed the rich in order to give the proceeds to the poor. But those original ballads in their entirety include only a single reference to an isolated incident of such charitable beneficence, which seems to stand as the lone foundation for the notion that this was Robin's standard MO. In fact, according to those ballads, neither Robin Hood nor Little John and the rest of the so-called Merry Men were the kind of people anyone would relish meeting on a dark night. 'Merry Men' is a corruption of the original Merrie Mein or Meinie with the first word then meaning fitting to the purpose – be that noble or unworthy – and the second denoting an entourage.

In 'Robin Hood and the Monk', first published in 1450 but known to have enjoyed oral popularity before that, Robin is recognized by one of his clerical victims when he ventures into Nottingham; the hue and cry raised by that monk results in Robin being trapped and arrested by the Sheriff's men. When they learn of this, Little John and Much the Miller's Son waylay the quisling monk and hack him to death before also killing a child who had witnessed their actions. As for Robin himself, on many occasions he is noted in early references to have mutilated his victims and captives by cutting off their noses and/or their ears, and, on one occasion, when he waylaid a party including a conjurer-juggler, the man annoyed him so much that he nailed him to a tree by his hands and left him to die.

People were then so much more at ease with the death of their heroes and, when it came time for Robin to quit the stage, these original ballads, including 'A Gest of Robyn

Hode', have him journey in diminished health to seek sanctuary with a prioress, who unfortunately gives him a slow poison to accelerate his death. Keeping him company to the end, Little John opens the window so that Robin can fire an arrow and, with his dying breath, he implores John to bury him wherever it falls. In the play *The Downfall of Robert Earl of Huntingdon*, the prioress is from Kirklees, and there is indeed a dedicated grave in the grounds of Kirklees Priory, which lies in West Yorkshire, not Nottinghamshire.

So, the original Robin Hood was a man of his medieval times, with the accounts of his adventures written for an audience of equal brutality who listened to such accounts

of his bloody deeds with amused admiration. Unsuited to the more delicate tastes of later centuries, all such references to Robin were swept under the carpet to remain equally obscure today. It is, in fact, the Robin of the sixteenth and seventeenth centuries who evolved into the Robin of modern cinema.

The elevation of Robin from the ranks of the peasantry or the yeomanry is first noted in *Chronicles at Large* (1569) by Richard Grafton, King's Printer under Henry VIII, the same source that first refers to Edward of Woodstock as the Black Prince but neglects to explain why. Grafton presents his Robin as an impoverished Earl who, having forfeited his estates and fortune through trumped-up charges of treason, is forced to go feral and live rough as a bandit. This new and more complex Robin of Grafton's *Chronicles* was further developed in the plays of Anthony Munday, who presented him as Robert, Earl of Huntingdon, who fell for the fair Maid Matilda in *The Downfall of Robert Earl of Huntingdon* (1598). Not only is this the first nod to any romance in the life of Robin but Matilda changes her name when she joins the outlaws to become Maid Marian in the second half of the drama. This play is thus the sole authority for the notion of a love triangle involving Robin, Marian and the evil Prince John, whose determination to wed the maid and acquire her birthright has become pivotal to so many modern depictions. So, it seems that in fact Robin was an ephemeral character, forced to morph with the changing mores. But could there have been a real man at the core of these legends?

Throughout the burgeoning tourist industry of the Victorian era, Yorkshire was apparently unconcerned by Nottingham making large the connection between Robin Hood and Sherwood Forest. Yorkshire had the Dales and the significant attraction of the spas of Harrogate to keep its tills ringing. Only in more recent times, with over 500,000 people a year visiting Nottingham to tour Sherwood, did Yorkshire start the battle to reclaim its native son. And, if there was a real person at the core of the legend, then there is much to suggest he came from that northern county.

Just five miles to the south of Whitby lies the picturesque fishing village of Robin Hood's Bay, known as such since the early fourteenth century. In 1324 Louis I, Count of Flanders, sent the first of many letters of complaint to Edward III, protesting the acts of piracy routinely visited upon Flemish fishing vessels, which were taken by force to be deprived of their catch by the village residents. The earliest reference to anyone called Robin Hood appears in the records of the legal proceedings of the York Assizes, dated 1225, which detail the confiscation of property to the value of 32 shillings and 6 pence from a person variously referred to as Robin Hood or Hod, to recover debts owed to the estates of the church of St Peter, prior to his being banished as an outlaw.

According to David Baldwin, Fellow of the Royal Historical Society and the specialist in medieval history who predicted that Richard III lay buried under the Greyfriars car park in Leicester nearly thirty years before

LINCOLN GREEN

Although it seems to make sense for forest-dwelling bandits to wear green clothing, and over the centuries there have been numerous references to 'Robin' wearing outfits cut from a cloth known as Lincoln Green, this is in fact a misunderstanding based on some very confusing terminology. Although the city of Lincoln did become famous for a green cloth, there is no reference to this Lincoln Green before 1510, which is a bit late for Robin to have been wearing it.

The cloth for which Lincoln *was* famous in Robin's time was a bright red weave called Lincoln Greyne, sometimes Grene, a name built on the fact that 'grenes', or grains, of red kermine dye — later called carmine — were used to achieve this well-fixed scarlet hue, which made the cloth both expensive and desirable.

Old references to Robin wearing Lincoln Grene or Lincoln Greyne were misunderstood by later readers who, by then aware of the popularity of the early sixteenth-century Lincoln Green, presumed 'grene' or 'greyne' to be archaic forms of 'green'.

this proved correct, the more likely son of York at the core of the legend would have been Roger Godberd, an outlaw known to have been active in Sherwood in the late 1260s. With the Great North Way that connected London and

York running straight through Sherwood Forest – which was not endless woodland but open rough country ('forest' in such times denoted a royal hunting ground) – this well-travelled route was a magnet for the likes of Godberd. As in the legend of Robin Hood, he led a gang of thugs who variously robbed and murdered travellers and churchmen in Sherwood, poached the king's deer and was once captured by the Sheriff of Nottingham, only to later escape. Many of the early ballads state that Robin Hood was driven into outlawry after his support for the abortive rebellion of 1263 led against Henry III by Simon de Montfort – and Godberd is known to have been such a supporter before having to take to the hills himself. The legendary Robin is closely associated with Loxley in South Yorkshire – he is even referred to as Robin of Loxley – and Godberd is buried in Loxley, Warwickshire, which could be a further confused connection.

Given Baldwin's predictive record when it comes to medieval characters and their fates, the smart money has to be on Godberd but, with Yorkshire considering its next move, the Nottingham/Sherwood bandwagon rolls on regardless.

———◇———

2

Voyages of Discovery

THE BOOK OF MARVELS: MARCO POLO'S CHINESE WHISPERS

M OST OF WHAT we know – or think we know – about Marco Polo comes to us as a hand-me-down from the old charlatan himself and his travelogue/memoirs published as *Il Milione* (The Million), a title that early sceptics chose to render as 'The Million Lies'. Claiming to have just returned from a protracted stay in China, Polo resurfaced in Venice, right in the middle of that city's war with Genoa, and was probably captured by the Genoese in 1296 off the Anatolian coast. He claimed to have dictated his book, now more usually referred to as *The Travels of Marco Polo*, to fellow inmate Rustichello da Pisa, captured by the Genoese back in 1284 and a well-known writer of romantic adventure. If that is so, then it is surprising in the extreme that only eighteen sentences in the entire manuscript are in the first person but, all such debate aside, the book, which is still in print, made Polo a great deal of money.

Provoking controversy from the outset, Polo's book still polarizes academic debate with the likes of Frances Wood, head of the Chinese Department at the British Library until 2013, prominent in the 'he-never-went-to-China' camp.

Her book detailing such argument, *Did Marco Polo Go to China?* (1995), still draws counter-arguments from other sinologists of equal standing such as Professors Morris Rossabi and Hans Vogel of the universities of Columbia in the United States and Tübingen in Germany respectively. And it must be said that Rossabi and Vogel are far from alone in their support for the claims of Polo who, as one might expect, waved aside all negative comment in his time and, as he lay dying, averred: 'I did not write half of what I saw, for I knew I would not be believed.' This is doubtless one of those historical conundrums to which there will never be a definitive answer.

Allegedly born into a family of prosperous Venetian traveller-traders, at the ripe old age of seventeen and in the company of his father Niccolò and his uncle Maffeo, Marco set off to China in 1271 where he claims they became the first Europeans to be granted admission to the court of the Khan, who in this case was Kublai Khan. The Mongol warlord had that very same year extended his grip on what is now northern China, completing his conquest of the rest of China in 1279 to establish the Yuan Dynasty. Marco tells us he became such a trusted confidant of Kublai Khan that, bearing a replica of the Khan's personal seal, he travelled far and wide to conduct various diplomatic missions. Still in his twenties, he claims to have acted as intermediary between the Khan and Pope Gregory X, after the former developed an interest in Christianity, and to have held the governorship of the city of Yangzhou for three years.

If indeed the Polos made it that far, they would not have been the first Europeans or even the first Italians to have stood before a Khan. In 1246, eight years before Marco was even born, Giovanni da Pian del Carpine, from Umbria in central Italy, was already standing before Güyük Khan, grandson of Genghis Khan, with a message of goodwill from Pope Innocent IV. Refusing Carpine's entreaties for him to embrace Christianity, Güyük instead told him that he expected the Pope and all Western leaders to swear allegiance to him. He then sent Carpine packing with a letter, triplicate in Mongol, Arabic and Latin, to tell Innocent IV as much in no uncertain terms. In 1254, the very year of Marco's birth, the Flemish explorer/missionary William of Rubruck met with both Batu Khan and Möngke Khan before returning to publish his forty-chapter book, *The Journey of William of Rubruck to the Eastern Parts of the World*, which, a bestseller in its time, is still recognized as a masterpiece of medieval geographical literature. Indeed, it was likely that it was the financial success of this book that encouraged Polo himself to venture into publishing.

Polo also grossly overstates the wealth and prominence of his family in Venice. While Marco did later acquire some considerable wealth for himself, it is clear that his family were small-time trader-dealers. As to his claims of having played the go-between for the Khan and the Pope, neither the records in China nor those of the Vatican indicate any such contact; likewise, the chronicles of Yangzhou fail to mention his governorship.

FROM CROATIA TO VENICE

In keeping with all the smoke and mirrors surrounding the life of Marco Polo, it is hardly surprising that no one is quite sure where his family originated. It has been suggested by some sources that they moved to Venice from what is today Croatia.

Some historians maintain the family were originally merchants of Korčula, an island that today forms part of Croatia but which in the thirteenth century was part of the former Venetian Republic. The family, originally named Pilić, moved to Venice and Latinized their name to Polo as both 'pilić' and 'polo' have etymological links to words denoting a chicken in Croatian and Italian respectively.

In the town of Korčula itself, there is a house purporting to be the original family home; it is currently under the protection of the local administration, which has plans to turn it into a museum.

Even his accounts of his alleged journeys around China raise serious questions, as the times taken to complete such trips fail to correspond with known distances between any two points cited and the duration of others' well-documented journeys. Also, despite his claims of having remained in China for over seventeen years, he failed to demonstrate the remotest familiarity with any language spoken in the Khan's realm of the day, making it unlikely that he would have been able to conduct the many diplomatic discussions of which he claimed to have been part. Furthermore, in his book he makes exclusive use of Persian names for Chinese locations instead of using those favoured by the locals.

There also seem to be some gaps in his knowledge when it comes to the locations of key places in China. Despite his claims of living in Fujian, the centre of both the manufacture of porcelain and the production of books by means of the early Chinese block-printing technique, his descriptions are chaotic and misinformed. He maintains that the production of such fine china is located in the non-existent city of Tingui, while the use of block-printing – way before its time in Europe – gets nary a mention. Nor indeed does the Chinese top-to-bottom-and-right-to-left writing style, which developed from the earliest of Chinese records being inscribed on bamboo poles. It has also been noted that nowhere in the book does Polo mention the stir-fry cooking styles favoured by the masses for whom coal was too expensive and firewood in short supply, this requiring them to dice their food before cooking it in what is now called a wok held over a small fire for a short duration. Nor does he remark on the striking similarity between Italian pasta and ravioli and the Chinese staple of noodles and small dumplings filled with spiced and ground meat.

By then, the drinking of tea had been ritualized by the Chinese, yet that beverage too is ignored. This is especially odd as the Chinese of the time tended not to entertain at home, officials preferring to honour guests with a visit to their favourite teahouse. As Marco himself was allegedly an official of the Khan, he would have been the recipient of countless such invitations from other officials – who would have expected reciprocation – and the elaborate ceremony surrounding the preparing, serving and drinking of tea would have been impossible for someone in his supposed position to miss. Despite the Great Wall of China running to the north of Yangzhou, the city he claims to have governed, this massive monument too evades his pen, which is doubly surprising since one of his journeys across China allegedly took him along the Silk Road, which would have required him to pass through one of the Great Wall's more impressive gates. He also fails to mention foot-binding, chopsticks, ice cream and the stunning spectacle of locals using trained cormorants to dive and catch fish for them in the river right outside the palace of the Khan. While this parasitic symbiosis between man and bird still amazes visitors to this day, Polo's pen remained unmoved.

Polo also makes elaborate mention of the Great Bridge of Beijing, allegedly having stood before it to count each of its twenty-four arches. Yet the bridge never had more than half that number of arches. There are similar problems with his account of his visit to the city of Suzhou in Jiangsu Province. The city was famed for being the most beautiful in China, with its unique styles of architecture drawing gasps from all who saw it. Polo, on the other hand, casually dismisses the place with a one-line reference to its being a renowned centre for the distribution of ginger and rhubarb, a trade to which the majestic city never stooped.

One of the more troubling in Polo's catalogue of historical errors is his claim to have brought Italian know-how to the aid of the Khan by showing him how to build huge catapults to bring his siege of Xiangyang to a successful conclusion. Although such machines were indeed used to break that siege, Chinese records show them to have been built by Persian engineers and the conflict at Xiangyang to have been over for a full year before Polo claims to have first entered the country. Also on the military front, Polo claims to have personally witnessed the departure of both fleets sent against Japan by the Khan in 1274 and again in 1281. Describing the ships of the fleets as being five-masted (they only had three), he laments the destruction of the first by a typhoon not far off the Japanese coast. In fact, this was the fate of the fleet of 1281 with the grateful Japanese hailing the typhoon as Kamikaze, or Divine Wind.

So, with his name appearing nowhere in any Chinese records of the period, the likelihood of Marco Polo having ever set foot in the country stands remote at best; many historians contend that he got no further than the Black Sea where, involved in the lucrative trade from countries further east, he simply picked the brains of those with whom he dealt.

Typical of the old rogue, even the date of his death remains elusive, as Venetian law of the time decreed the day to end with the setting of the sun, so whether he died on 8 or 9 January 1324 is unclear. Suffering ill-health in the closing months of 1323, Polo put all his affairs in order, his will leaving handsome bequests to family members and various religious institutes; he further declared that all debts to him and his estate should be regarded as void. It is of interest that, with the Vatican then entitled to a percentage of everyone's estate upon their passing, beady-eyed and avaricious clerics drew up a very detailed inventory of all his possessions. Yet in that meticulous listing there is not one item that would have connected the owner to China. Is it conceivable that he could have spent seventeen years in a country as fascinatingly different to medieval Europe as China without bringing home a single item of Chinese origin?

———◦———

AMERICA: WHO GOT
THERE FIRST?

SCHOOLS – ESPECIALLY THOSE in the United States – still teach that the Genoese explorer Christopher Columbus, under commission to the Spanish throne, discovered America in 1492 and that the continent was named after his contemporary, Amerigo Vespucci. In the States, where 'Columbus' is used to name everything from towns to space missions, they still make much of the man, which is surprising as he never even made it to their shores.

Paradoxically, it was in fact the Russians who were the first to 'discover' America when Siberian tribes simply wandered across the land that connected Russia to Alaska some 20,000 years ago. Next to pip Columbus to the post were probably the Ainu, the original and indigenous Japanese of Hokkaido, who may have in turn been driven out by the smaller yet far more aggressive Polynesians. (The Ainu lived in Siberia, too, so they may also have simply migrated from there.) Also beating Columbus to the post were the Vikings under Leif Erikson.

Unlike Columbus – who actually made four voyages of limited discovery, reaching as far as the Caribbean and the coast of Central America – Amerigo Vespucci, a Florentine explorer under commission to Portugal, claimed to have made four voyages to the New World but only made two: his first and fourth voyages only happened in his head. In his 'second' and 'third' voyages – in reality his first and second – of 1499 and 1501 respectively, Vespucci did indeed venture further than the Caribbean to encounter the north coast of South America and to have then followed the east coast as far south as the Bay of Rio de Janeiro; he claimed to have travelled as far south as what is now Patagonia but, as he was a notorious liar, no one believed him. Based on Vespucci's notes and charts, the German cartographer Martin Waldseemüller produced a map of South America in 1507, this being the earliest use of the name 'America', which Waldseemüller's notes say he assumes to have been inspired by the forename of Vespucci. This would suggest that he had seen the name on other maps of the New World and thus decided to follow suit but, significantly, in his later issues of that map he replaced 'America' with 'Terra Incognita'.

The far more likely toponymous hero is the otherwise little-known Robert Amerike, a wealthy Bristolian merchant who sponsored the voyages of John Cabot, providing the ship *Matthew* in which John Cabot reached Labrador in May 1497. Pre-dating any visit to the New World made by Vespucci by over two years, Cabot explored the North American coastline from Nova Scotia to Newfoundland and, in the time-honoured tradition, no doubt applied a form of his sponsor's surname to the land.

The weight of tradition also lends support to this notion in that toponymous honours are rarely based on the forename of any explorer or sponsor. When Henry Hudson discovered a new river in what is now New York in the early seventeenth century he did not, for example, call it Henry's River but the Hudson; had the toponymous honour been heaped upon the unworthy shoulders of Amerigo Vespucci then the New World would have been called Vespuccia and not America. But that is enough of those who did *not* make it to North America; what of those who did?

Following those Siberians some 10,000 years later, the first to travel to the New World instead of stumble into it were the Ainu, the indigenous people of northern Japan and Siberia. Japan is not that far from Alaska, which, with its chain of Aleutian Islands stretching well beyond the 180-degree meridian separating the western and eastern hemispheres, qualifies as the most northern, western and eastern of the American states. The furthest flung island of that chain, Attu, lies about 1,000 miles from Alaska proper and about the same distance from Japan to form the first rung of an island ladder to the North American mainland. Debate as to whether the indigenous Japanese had paddled across to Attu or whether Siberian Ainu had crossed over the northern land bridge was brought to a head on 28 July 1996 with the discovery of an almost complete skeleton in the Lake Wallula section of the Columbia River in Kennewick, Washington State. With carbon dating establishing an age of about 9,000 years, it was discovered that the ancestry of Kennewick Man most closely resembled that of the Ainu.

The North American Graves Protection and Repatriation lobby demanded Kennewick Man be released into their custody for tribal burial. The anthropological and paleontological groups, aware that such a move would forever mark Kennewick Man as a Native American and place him beyond their attempts to get to the bottom of a mystery, pressured the government to resist any such move. Caught in the middle, the government took refuge in the fact that the land on which the remains had been found belonged to the US Army so they should retain custody, a move which pleased nobody. A victory of sorts for all was provided in 2015 by the University of Copenhagen, which, through DNA testing, asserted that the remains presented conclusive similarities to the Native American tribes of Washington State so there was indeed a link. But with the Ainu having been in America for over 9,000 years this was a double-edged statement; with the inevitable intermingling of all early peoples on the continent one would expect to find genetic similarities in trace DNA in tribes local to where Kennewick Man was found. After all, he is unlikely to have pitched up there on his own. So, the University of Copenhagen only answered half of the question with no indication as to which group was there first.

Next to settle and colonize North America were tenth-century Vikings, the very first Europeans in America. Striking out from their powerbase on Greenland, a small fleet of long ships, under the command of Leif Erikson, landed on the northern tip of Newfoundland in AD 1000 to establish a settlement at what is now L'Anse aux Meadows. From here, it is thought that the Vikings moved to the North American mainland where, across the next couple of decades, they established more settlements, with the most recent find of 2017 uncovering what may be a Viking village at Minisceongo Creek, near the Hudson River in New York State, thus proving the Vikings extended their influence as far south as New England. This was nearly half a millennium before Columbus didn't make it to America so the real mystery is how he managed to grab all the kudos – and the answer to that lies in transatlantic hostilities between the UK and the emerging USA.

A SHORTCUT TO INDIA

Columbus was not much of a navigator; he thought the world to be about half the size it really was and, with this misconception foremost in his mind, when he sailed west in 1492 it was with the intention of finding a shortcut to India and the east. When he arrived in the Caribbean he was convinced he was in India, hence nonsensical names such as the West Indies and the Native Americans also being called Indians.

As for the notion that his voyage proved the earth round and not flat, this was the invention of American humorist Washington Irving in his *A History of the Life and Voyages of Christopher Columbus* (1828), in which the author asserted that the Spanish Council of Salamanca opposed the funding of Columbus's voyage on the grounds that he would sail off the edge and perish.

In fact, none then thought the world flat and the Council of Salamanca only questioned Columbus's estimates of the size of the world. As things turned out, they were right and he was wrong.

After the 1775–83 conflict called the American War of Independence or the American Revolution, depending on which side of the Atlantic you sit, the United States wanted nothing to do with anyone or anything English. Words such as 'master' were ousted in favour of the Dutch-derived 'boss' and any man foolish enough to appear in public sporting a powdered wig risked hostility ranging from the verbal to the physical. Oblivious to the past discoveries of the Siberians, ethnic Japanese and Vikings in post-revolutionary America, it was a straight toss-up between the non-English Columbus and the English-funded John Cabot and, despite the former not even making it to their shores, Columbus was the clear winner. To further disassociate themselves from the hated British during the War of Independence, the American revolutionaries referred to their country as the Territory of Columbus or Columbia, thus the name 'District of Columbia' given to the land set aside for their new post-war capital of Washington where Congress held its first meeting at the turn of the nineteenth century. This new Congress, desperate to distance itself from the British Crown with a new national identity, promoted Columbus as a man who sailed west in an effort to shrug off the old world order and, like their own fledgling nation, sought an independent future. Anything and everything was 'Columbified'; King's College in New York, founded by Royal Charter by George II in 1754, was renamed Columbia University and, after the war, 'Hail Columbia' by Joseph Hopkinson became the country's de facto national anthem to be sung on the tricentenary of Columbus's 1492 voyage – the new country's first national celebrations.

With Cabot and all the other contenders thus airbrushed from the American perspective of their own foundation, the

Columbus bandwagon kept rolling, picking up momentum from the likes of the Catholic order of the Knights of Columbus, a 'muscular Christian' group founded in the United States in the 1800s who succeeded in establishing 12 October as Columbus Day. But, as more became aware of the atrocities inflicted by Columbus, eventually sent home in chains for his crimes of slaughter and enslavement against the peoples of the islands he actually *did* discover, the gilt started to peel from that particular bit of gingerbread. To take Haiti as one example, when Columbus arrived in 1492 there was a healthy population of around 500,000 Arawaks; two years later over half were either dead or elsewhere in chains. This, combined with an increasing awareness of the mass rapes and mutilation imposed by Columbus on communities that failed to render his required levy of gold, prompted a recent yet steady abandonment of any celebrations of his memorial day across America. At present, twenty-one of the states ignore the festival completely and, of the remaining twenty-nine states, the overwhelming majority now choose to observe 12 October as Indigenous Peoples' Day. In 1964, Congress made formal submission to President Lyndon B. Johnson, requiring him to declare 9 October as Leif Erikson Day and, at the time of writing, there was a sizeable demonstration mounted by New Yorkers calling on their mayor, Bill de Blasio, to remove Columbus's statue from Central Park.

—◇—

COOKING UP A LIE:
WHO REALLY DISCOVERED
AUSTRALIA?

WHEN IT COMES to hailing an explorer as the first to set foot on any landmass, what the history books really mean – especially British history books – is who was the first white guy to get there. Ask anyone at random who discovered Australia and the chances are they will confidently reply 'Captain Cook', but the first and true discoverers of the Australian continent were African travellers who beat him to it by over 40,000 years. The Australian Aborigines are living descendants of Africans who migrated from their homeland and, as their DNA proves, intermingled on their way through India, Malaysia and Borneo until they pitched up on Timor to complete the last 650 miles of their journey on primitive rafts to land on Australia's northern coast.

The ancient Chinese made frequent visits to Australia as evidenced by mention in 338 BC of the Imperial Zoo of Peking exhibiting kangaroos and the existence of a 2,000-year-old Chinese vase bearing a map of the eastern Australian coastline. The first full-scale Chinese exploration of Australia was conducted in 1422 by Admiral Zheng, who divided his fleet to explore the east and west coast of the continent simultaneously. And before the Chinese came hunter-traders from many other parts of Asia who, visiting about 5,000 years ago, brought with them their domesticated hunting dogs, some of which escaped to go feral and evolve into the dingo we know today. Next, and a long way down the list, came the Europeans with the first being the otherwise little-known Willem Janszoon (1570–1630), a Dutchman who sailed into what is now called the Gulf of Carpentaria to drop anchor on 26 February 1606 on the Pennefather River on the western shore of Cape York in northern Australia. Establishing a makeshift settlement, he began charting hundreds of miles of the coastline but was eventually forced to abandon his settlement due to what he claimed to have been inexplicable hostility from the locals. Local oral tradition, on the other hand, records the hostilities having been due to the Dutch interlopers kidnapping local women and trying to force the men into hunting and labouring for them.

Next came the Dutchman Dirk Hartog who, in 1616, sailed into the Shark's Bay area of Western Australia; he was the first to recognize Australia as a continent and not merely the island presumed by Janszoon. In 1644, the Dutchman Abel Tasman, the man who gave his name to Tasmania, explored and charted most of Australia's northern coastline – so the Dutch had been charting and establishing settlements in the land they called New Holland a century before James Cook (1728–79) was even born. Australians certainly recognize Janszoon as the first European to make

CAPTAIN JAMES COOK

Although he could not lay claim to the discovery of Australia, James Cook was the foremost explorer, cartographer and navigator of the eighteenth century, and made three important voyages of discovery. On his last and fateful voyage, between 1776 and 1779, he became the first European to make contact with the natives on Hawaii. Suspecting the Hawaiians of stealing supplies and possibly a longboat, Cook marched ashore to take the king of the island hostage, only to be clubbed to death along with other members of his shore party. Cook's body was pit-roasted on the beach with the bones later returned to his crew on HMS *Resolution* for burial at sea.

it to their shores, commemorating his landing with a replica of his ship, *Duyfken* (Little Dove), currently in Perth.

The first Englishman to take any interest in the new Dutch acquisition was the truculent pirate/privateer William Dampier (1651–1715) who, after landing near King Sound on the western coast, returned to London to report his findings to the Admiralty. In January 1699 he was given command of HMS *Roebuck* and sent back to chart 900 miles of the western coast, so claims that nobody in Britain was aware of Australia's existence before Cook's voyage of 1768 are ridiculous.

In that year Lieutenant (not Captain) Cook was hired by the Royal Society to make for Tahiti and record the transit of Venus over that island, predicted for 3 June 1769; that done, he was to continue south-westward to check out New Zealand, first explored and charted by Abel Tasman in 1642–3, and establish whether it was insular or continental. All of this Cook completed with typical diligence and attention to detail to prove that Tasman's discovery was indeed insular and not part of the Australian continent. Next, and of his own volition, Cook set sail for the southern tip of Australia's east coast, which he sighted on 19 April 1770, before following that coastline north to narrowly avoid the total loss of his ship on the Great Barrier Reef. That Cook was an intrepid navigator and a meticulous cartographer is beyond dispute, but how he managed to wrest the accolade of Australia's discovery from the Dutch is itself a mystery – or is it? The British of the time were in serious competition and frequently at war with the Dutch so they simply 'cooked' the history books to shoehorn Cook into the discovery seat and airbrush the Dutch out of the picture. Their only other possible candidate was the bumptious pirate William Dampier and he would never do. He wasn't even an officer of the Royal Navy. But Dampier does at least have one other claim to fame, as it was his notoriously foul temper that was ultimately responsible for inspiring *Robinson Crusoe* (1719).

In 1704, having returned to his piratical ways, Dampier was sailing in partnership with Thomas Stradling, captain of the *Cinque Ports*, and in command of the *St George* off

the coast of Chile. Dampier's temper caused a rift in the
partnership and the two ships ended up going their own
ways, causing hostility between Stradling and his leading
crewman, Alexander Selkirk, who had run away to sea to
avoid prosecution in Fife for indecency in a churchyard,
no less. In a fit of pique, Selkirk demanded to be put
ashore at next landfall, which just happened to be the
deserted island of Juan Fernández, his home for the next
five years. When Captain Woodes Rogers of the *Duke*
dropped anchor on 1 February 1709 in search of fresh
water, Selkirk's initial joy at his salvation soon abated: as
the *Duke*'s longboat neared the ship, he could see his old
friend Dampier snarling over the side. At first, Selkirk
demanded that he should be taken back to his island but,

eventually placated, he boarded the *Duke* for return to England, where his tale helped inspire Daniel Defoe to pen his classic.

———◄◊►———

MAN AND MYTH: BLIGH'S MUTINY ON THE BOUNTY

Portrayed in countless movies and dramas as the demented sadist in command of a ship called HMS *Bounty*, William Bligh was not a captain of advancing years but a thirty-four-year-old lieutenant in charge of a converted merchantman called HMAV (His Majesty's Armed Vessel) *Bounty*. The *Bounty* was dispatched to Tahiti in 1787 to collect samples of breadfruit to see if it would provide a cheap and sustainable resource to feed slaves in the West Indies. The traditional perception of the regime aboard that ship is one of Bligh treating the vessel as his personal and sadistic fiefdom in which the crew, protected to a certain degree by the noble first mate, Fletcher Christian, suffered humiliations and punishments until Christian, unable to exert any restraint on the increasingly unhinged Bligh, was reluctantly forced to lead the men in the most famous mutiny in the history of the British Navy.

In reality, Fletcher Christian was something of a petulant fop with ideas above his station. He had sailed under Bligh before and was keen to join his expedition to Tahiti. Equally keen to have him along for the ride, Bligh submitted a written request to the Navy Board suggesting

Christian be appointed Master's Mate for the trip, but the board, concerned at Christian's lack of seniority and length of service, appointed one John Fryer to that position. Halfway through the voyage and concerned at Fryer's lack of efficiency, Bligh replaced him with Christian, whom he further promoted to Acting Lieutenant, so it can be inferred from that alone that there was no bad blood between the two at the time.

As for Bligh being possessed of a sadistic streak that afforded him something akin to homoerotic thrills from seeing men lashed within an inch of their lives, this too is nonsense. Several of the aforementioned cinematic character assassinations also show him keel-hauling his men but that practice – which involved tying a miscreant

to a rope and dragging him under the keel of the ship, from one side to the other, while it was under way – had been abandoned by the Royal Navy in about 1720, decades before either Christian or Bligh had even been born.

In fact, all the records and testimony of those who elected to throw in their lot with Bligh during the mutiny reveal him to have been excessively lenient for his day, only resorting to the lash when absolutely necessary. Frequently on that expedition, he had given up his cabin to men coming off watch soaking wet and frozen – hardly the action of a sadistic brute. While carrying out their mission to harvest breadfruit from Tahiti, most of the men were seduced by the friendly paradise and the openly permissive attitude to sex held by the local girls – so much so that three of the crew, Charles Churchill, John Millward and William Muspratt, deserted and hid in order to remain after the *Bounty* had sailed. When they were captured, Bligh, sympathetic to the temptations that had prompted their actions, only gave them the lash; any other commander of his day would have strung them up from the yardarm. In general, the log of the *Bounty* clearly demonstrates that Bligh issued rebukes for shortcomings that would have had almost any other commander reaching for the lash, and he invariably resorted to corporal punishment for crimes that would normally have incurred a death sentence.

So, why today do we suffer from the misperception of Bligh as the beastly villain and Christian as a man reluctantly driven to mutiny to save the crew from his tyranny? The answer to that lies in the efforts of the Christian family and that of another equally well-connected mutineer, Peter Heywood.

On 28 April 1789, with the *Bounty* twenty-four days into her homeward journey and the lure of the lifestyle in Tahiti still so fresh in the men's minds, Christian led about half of the crew in a bloodless takeover of the ship. With Bligh appealing to his friend to be reasonable and think of what he was about to do, Christian could only repeat, over and over again, 'I am in Hell,' as he paced the deck. So, perhaps the kindest interpretation one could place on his mutiny is that it resulted from his having some sort of breakdown; Bligh himself would later state that Christian had been in a 'state of fugue' throughout. Those who survived the subsequent and abortive settlement of Pitcairn Island by the mutineers certainly recalled his violent mood swings and that he spent a lot of time alone in his favourite cave, where he could be heard either crying or laughing maniacally.

Be that as it may, Bligh and eighteen of the forty-two-strong crew were bundled into the *Bounty*'s longboat with limited supplies, instruments and the ship's log – but no charts – and then set adrift. Other crew members who had expressed a desire to remain loyal were told by Bligh there was no room for them in the boat so they should remain with the *Bounty*, secure in his promise that he would speak for them should he make it back to England. Basically left for dead, Bligh navigated that longboat the

ANOTHER MUTINY

Few are aware that William Bligh was central to another and much larger mutiny in Australia after his appointment as Governor of New South Wales in 1805. He was under orders to crack down on the illegal rum trade in the colony. With his ill-deserved reputation as the Bastard of the *Bounty* preceding him, none in Australia relished his arrival. The settlers and even the New South Wales Corps (the troops supposedly under the control of the governor) were all doing very well out of the rum-running that they knew he was coming to crush.

Bligh attacked the problem head on, which brought him into immediate conflict with John Macarthur, Sydney's leading citizen, whose protestations at Bligh's strict policies resulted in a warrant being issued for his arrest. Instead of acting on this, the Corps, under the command of Major George Johnston, a close friend of Macarthur and fellow rum-runner, marched on the Governor's House to arrest Bligh instead.

After a short period of confinement, Bligh returned to the UK with few reprisals, if any, being visited on the mutineers.

3,600 miles to Timor using only a sextant, his pocket watch and the stars. Completed in forty-seven days, this is still internationally recognized as the most remarkable feat of navigation in maritime history. Given a hero's welcome on his return to Britain in 1790, Bligh was cleared of any responsibility for the loss of the *Bounty* by a board of inquiry and returned to duty to immediately undertake his so-called Second Breadfruit Journey. Returning to Tahiti, his mission this time was to take breadfruit to the West Indies before returning with samples of ackee fruit, which the Royal Society named *Blighia sapida* in his honour.

Another strong indication as to the state of Christian's mind at the time is the fact that he hadn't a clue what to do next; he simply had not thought it through. Meeting with a hostile reception on a couple of islands, the mutineers eventually returned to Tahiti where Heywood and a dozen others elected to remain while Christian, keen to have servants and sexual diversion, lured aboard eighteen Tahitians – six men and twelve women – under false promise of a party, but instead set sail for Pitcairn Island. To be fair, this was a canny choice of bolthole. Although named after Robert Pitcairn, who first spotted it in 1767 (his father, Major John Pitcairn, had been the man in charge of the British troops at Lexington, Massachusetts, when the first shots of the American War of Independence were fired), Christian knew it to be either incorrectly indicated or completely missing from Admiralty charts.

As the Christian contingent of mutineers and their kidnapped Tahitians dug in on Pitcairn, HMS *Pandora* arrived at Tahiti to arrest Heywood and the others who had chosen to remain there. At first Heywood tried to bluff his way, rowing out to greet the warship enthusiastically, informing the officers that he had been one of the unfortunate men who, although loyal to Bligh, had been excluded from the longboat and bundled below decks. It might have worked too but onto the deck stepped Lt Thomas Hayward who, having made the Timor journey with Bligh, informed his captain that Heywood had been on deck and beside Christian throughout the affair. By the time of Heywood's trial in September 1792, Hayward was deployed on the other side of the world and so, with his continued perjury thus left unchallenged and with his family's relentless campaign, Heywood was pardoned and avoided the rope that claimed his co-defendants.

From this point on, the Christian and Heywood families, with ties to each other and many strings to pull between them, campaigned tirelessly to salvage their own reputations and those of their sons by blackening that of Bligh. Heywood was presented as a man of sensitivity who, although understanding of the mutineers' motives, remained steadfastly loyal to his demonic captain, while Christian was likewise painted as a man driven to the unthinkable by the tyrannical bestiality of a megalomaniac on the brink of homicidal actions. Although this was scoffed at within the Admiralty, the court of public opinion lapped it up to such a degree that this is still very much the modern perception, consistently reinforced by cinematic portrayals of Bligh as the gimlet-eyed sadist while Christian is played by charismatic 'hunks' such as Marlon Brando or, more recently, Mel Gibson. In reality, Christian was described as being of short stature, dark and swarthy with an 'unpleasantly sweaty aspect, especially his hands which soiled all they touched'.

Once ensconced on Pitcairn, the mutineers reverted to type, treating the Tahitian males like slaves and the women like sex objects and, eventually, it was the women who led the mutiny against Christian and his cohorts, murdering most of them in their sleep.

Unbelievably, consequences of the Christian–Bligh feud have rolled on for another 225 years. Brenda Christian, who took over as Mayor of Pitcairn after her brother, Steve, was incarcerated for the rape of minors, was so incensed by the opinions that Dea Birkett, author of *Serpent in Paradise* (1997), expressed about Christian and the mutineers' descendants, that she said, 'I'd like to see her hanged.' Birkett said in 2014, 'Even now I wouldn't risk going to Pitcairn if my last name were Bligh.' Sydney-based celebrity chef Glynn Christian likewise threatened to punch Maurice Bligh in the face for making uncomplimentary remarks about Fletcher Christian on Australian television. However, in May 2004, Jacqui Christian travelled to Tahiti to meet Maurice Bligh and return to him William Bligh's Bible, which had been stolen from his cabin during the mutiny. Maurice then symbolically gave the book back to Jacqui so it could be returned to Pitcairn for ever. And there, for the time being at least, the matter rests.

———◄o►———

GHOST SHIP: THE MYSTERIOUSLY ABANDONED MARY CELESTE

THE KNOWN FACTS surrounding the abandonment of the *Mary Celeste* on the high seas call for a lot less speculation and eye-rolling than the embellishments of the event heaped upon that same vessel under her more mysterious but erroneous name of Marie Celeste.

Built at Spencer's Island, Nova Scotia, and first named *Amazon*, the ship later renamed *Mary Celeste* was launched on 18 May 1861 against the backdrop of the American Civil War and, to be fair, she does seem to have been a ship of ill omen. Her first captain and part-owner, Robert McLellan, fell ill and died while supervising her loading for the maiden voyage to London, which was undertaken instead by one Captain John Nutting Parker. On the outward-bound leg of that journey, *Amazon* crashed into a fishing dam in the straits off the state of Maine and, on the return leg, she crashed into and sank a brig in the Strait of Dover. After successive owners had failed to make her pay, *Amazon* was – in rather suspicious circumstances – driven against the rocky coast of Cape Breton Island during some admittedly stormy weather in October 1867; the owners abandoned her as a wreck and walked away with the insurance money.

Next, the remains were bought by Richard Haines of New York who, having spent $9,000 returning her to a seaworthy condition and with a greater carrying capacity, re-registered her as the *Mary Celeste*, a name inspired by Maria Celeste, the illegitimate daughter of Galileo and his mistress, Marina Gamba.

In late October 1872 the *Mary Celeste* was at berth in New York's East River and being loaded with 1,701 barrels of raw commercial alcohol for transit to Genoa. With her cargo, valued at $35,000 and fully insured, she set sail on 7 November with her new captain and part-owner, Benjamin Briggs, at the helm; also on board were Briggs's wife and daughter and a crew of seven. On 4 December, the British-registered *Dei Gratia*, captained by David Morehouse, which had left New York a week later and was also bound for Genoa, came upon the *Mary Celeste* about

halfway between the Azores and Gibraltar. Still under reduced sail but making very unsteady passage through the water, the *Mary Celeste* appeared to Morehouse to be abandoned so he sent a small party across to see what was going on.

His first mate, Oliver Deveau, reported back that while there were no signs of violence or upheaval, no one was aboard, yet all personal possessions were in place; it appeared as though everyone had simply disappeared into thin air. As far as Deveau could ascertain, all the cargo was intact, yet all the covers to the hatches granting access to the hold had been removed as if someone had been trying to ventilate it. The ship's side rails next to the midship storage point of the longboat had been removed to facilitate the launch of that craft and the ship's sextant and marine chronometer were missing; also, one of the strong sail-ropes, the peak halyard, had been taken down and tied to the stern as if to tow the longboat behind for some reason. At a loss for anything better to do, Morehouse, who just happened to be a friend of Briggs, put a skeleton crew aboard the *Mary Celeste* and both ships made for Gibraltar, where they arrived on 12 and 13 December.

A court of inquiry was immediately convened with examination of the *Mary Celeste* revealing nothing out of the ordinary – apart from the fact that all ten aboard had disappeared. There was no internal or external damage to suggest what might have instigated such abandonment, which had obviously been undertaken in a hurried yet orderly manner. Nevertheless, the Attorney

General of Gibraltar, Frederick Solly-Flood, a pompous and arrogant man disliked by all, was determined to establish foul play; in fact, his wild imaginings were the very bedrock on which subsequent outlandish theories were founded. He first postulated that the crew must have got at the cargo and, in a drunken frenzy, murdered the captain and his family before taking off in the longboat. When it was pointed out that none of the barrels had been breached and their contents were quite undrinkable, Solly-Flood moved on to the stance that Captain Briggs must have murdered the crew and then waited for his friend, Morehouse, to catch up and complete their plot to claim the salvage money. He also suggested that Morehouse's decision to remain in Gibraltar to make himself available to the proceedings, while allowing his ship to continue to Genoa under Deveau, was simply a ruse to spirit away Briggs and his family, allegedly hidden aboard.

Having been unable to prove anything of the sort, Solly-Flood moved on to the ship having been attacked by a giant squid or octopus, or the entire crew having been sucked from the decks by a waterspout of outlandish proportion. Despite none of Solly-Flood's theories allowing for the hurried but professional evacuation of everyone into the ship's longboat, Gibraltar – not to mention Europe and America – was soon buzzing with tales of the ship having been attacked by a sea monster or by the *Flying Dutchman* ghost ship, rising up from the sea to spirit away all aboard.

THE BRIGGS FAMILY CURSE

The year before he set out on his ill-fated voyage on the *Mary Celeste*, Captain Benjamin Spooner Briggs had decided to give up the sea and almost bought a hardware store in New Bedford, Massachusetts. In hindsight, this would have been a wise move.

As a treat, Briggs decided to take his wife, Sarah, and their daughter, Sophia, along for the ride on the *Mary Celeste*, so they disappeared with him. Their son, Arthur, was left ashore with relatives as he was of school age. But tragedy was also to befall him in later life when he was struck and killed by a falling tree in a storm.

The rest of Briggs's family were no less unfortunate. His father was killed by lightning and his brother, Oliver, who had decided on a life in hardware after hearing of Benjamin's fate, went to sea just two months later. On 8 January 1873 Oliver's ship, the *Julia A. Hallock*, was struck by a sudden storm in the Bay of Biscay and sank in minutes, taking Oliver with it.

After no conclusions whatsoever were made as to the fate that had befallen the crew of the *Mary Celeste*, the ship was released to continue to Genoa under a Captain Blatchford, brought out from Boston by the ship's co-owners. Unfortunately for Morehouse, his reputation was forever stained by Solly-Flood's ravings, which also gave the insurers of the *Mary Celeste* the leeway to offer a derisory 20 per cent of the combined value of the ship and cargo as salvage money when the going rate was 50 per cent.

In all likelihood, the world would have forgotten about the *Mary Celeste* had it not been for a young Arthur Conan Doyle, then publishing anonymously. The January 1884 edition of the *Cornhill Magazine* published his short and darkly gothic version of the fate of those aboard the ship he renamed the *Marie Celeste*. Under the title of 'J. Habakuk Jephson's Statement', it is from this narrative that we inherit all the ghost-ship embellishments such as the half-eaten meals on the table with mugs of steaming tea and still-burning pipes laid carefully to one side. Presented as if dictated by the titular character, sole survivor of the demonic and homicidal insanity that overcame all others on board, many took the story to be factual. The *Boston Herald* certainly swallowed the yarn hook, line and sinker, reproducing it as a factual account to leave its readers under the impression that this had been the terrible fate of those aboard the *Mary Celeste*.

Modern science seems to have come up with the most logical explanation as to the fate of the ship and crew. When the ship was unloaded at Genoa, nine of the 1,701 wooden barrels of alcohol in the hold were found to be unbreached but empty. The other 1,692 barrels were made of white oak, but the empty ones were made of red oak, which, not having the occluded pores that make white oak watertight, is best suited to the storage of dry goods. The shippers of the cargo, Meissner, Ackermann & Co., had accidentally used nine barrels which, quite unsuitable for the storage of a volatile fluid, had allowed their contents to seep through their walls and fill the cargo hold with fumes. This would explain why the crew had removed the hatch covers granting access to the hold but, with alcohol fumes being much heavier than air, this would have done little to lessen the danger level of their situation. The dangerous nature of the cargo as the root cause of the evacuation had been explored before but always discounted as it was known that, when the ship had been examined on arrival at Gibraltar, there had been no signs anywhere on the ship of fire or explosion.

However, in 2006 Dr Andrea Sella, Professor of Chemistry at University College London and a man of international acclaim in his field, created a replica of the *Mary Celeste* cargo hold into which he packed paper cubes before flooding the compartment with butane and igniting it. One would expect this to result in crushed and charred cubes and scorched walls but nothing of the sort happened. As Sella explained, what he had created was a pressure-wave flash explosion which, although dramatic and frightening, occurred against a background of relatively cool air and was of such short duration as to leave neither structural damage nor signs of scorching or charring. And, Sella stressed, the alcohol fumes in the hold of the *Mary Celeste* would have flash-burned a lot faster and a lot colder than his butane. If this was indeed the cause of the evacuation, one can appreciate the panic produced among a crew who, acutely aware of the dangerous nature of their cargo, saw the hatches blown off by a violent rush of vivid flame from the cargo hold. Understandably reluctant to hang around for a repeat performance of such an event, Briggs and his crew took to the longboat, lashed in tow to the *Mary Celeste*, hoping for the best. Somehow the halyard had become detached from the cleats on the longboat to leave the party drifting to their doom. When Deveau went on board a few days later, all the alcohol fumes had flashed off, leaving no tell-tale odour.

Bad luck continued to dog the *Mary Celeste*. The 1880s saw her working West Indian waters, yet still with no one managing to run her at a profit; when three of her owner-captains died prematurely, she was branded a cursed ship. This allowed the shifty Gilman C. Parker to snap her up for a song – and he was a man who knew exactly how to make money out of the *Mary Celeste*. In November 1884 and in collusion with others, including his first mate, Parker crammed her to the gunwales with worthless junk – barrels supposedly filled with fine wine, which in fact contained water, and so forth – before driving her at full speed onto the Rochelais coral reef off the coast of Haiti. When he tried to claim the $30,000 insurance money – close to $1 million at today's values – he was instead told to expect prosecution for fraud, but both Parker and his first mate died before warrants could be issued: Parker choked to death in a drunken stupor and the first mate, Fillmore Tyson, came a very poor second in a knife fight. Parker's three other co-defendants fared no better:

one died, another was declared insane and the third shot himself, prompting the belief that the *Mary Celeste* had reached out from the bottom of the sea to bring down those who had destroyed her.

———◄○►———

WALKING WITHOUT LEGS:
THE MONOLITHS OF
EASTER ISLAND

FIRST SETTLED BY Polynesian adventurers around 700 AD, the island known to its present population as Rapa Nui successfully evaded contact with Europeans until Easter Sunday, 1722, when Dutch explorer Jacob Roggeveen blundered onto its shores while trying to make his way to Australia. What he found there was both depressing and intriguing – barren and desolate, the island was host to about 2,000 malnourished people and hundreds of strange-looking stone statues that have puzzled and exercised archaeological minds ever since.

The total number of Mo'ai, as the statues are known, including those unfinished at the quarry or broken and abandoned in transport, exceeds 1,100. The overwhelming majority of these are uniform in their height and weight – about 4 metres and 14 tons respectively – but there are a few much larger ones measuring up to 12 metres and weighing over 80 tons. All were carved from the considerable deposits of volcanic tuff at the centre of the island, tuff being a relatively soft rock formed by volcanic ash. The stones were raised up to honour the ancestors of whichever family was doing the carving or paying the sculptors, who used axes and chisels made of basalt, a much harder and igneous volcanic rock. So, no mystery surrounding why they were carved nor indeed how – the main bone of contention among archaeologists concerns how they were transported to their various positions about the island.

There were, of course, various theories as to how these monolithic statues were moved from the central quarry to stand like sullen sentinels about the shoreline of this isolated and triangular island, which measures about 14 miles long by 7 miles wide. Until recently, most people believed the statues had been moved from the quarry on sledges running over wooden rollers – but not everyone was satisfied with this seemingly logical assertion. In 2000, Charles Love, an archaeologist and anthropologist from Wyoming, conducted an extensive survey of the network of roadways radiating out from that central quarry and, having cleared away the accumulated dirt and dust to get down to the original road beds, he discovered they were all U-shaped – a mirror image of the modern road with its convex camber. The results of Love's survey punched a rather large hole in the sledge theory as rollers would have snapped through lack of central support from the countersunk road – indeed, if the intention was to use the sledge-and-roller method, then flat roads would have been laid. Love's discovery added the final link to a chain of thought being forged elsewhere.

In 2011 two men took themselves off to Easter Island to, quite literally, road-test their theory. One was Carl

Lipo, then Professor of Archaeology at the California State University, and the other was Terry Hunt, an archaeologist and anthropologist specializing in Pacific cultures. Both had been intrigued by the fact that the people of the island were united in their oral tradition that the statues had magically walked from the quarry to their site of installation; there were also several songs about 'walking the Mo'ai', which had a strong work-song rhythm like sea-shanties, themselves written to mark time and rhythm during rope hauling. The Rapa Nui language even includes the expression '*neke-neke*', which means 'walking without legs'; rather intriguingly, in the Maori language '*neke*' denotes a snake. When an islander called Leonardo Haoa Pakomio had previously been asked by ethnologist and adventurer Thor Heyerdahl to demonstrate *neke-neke*, the old man stood up and, holding his arms to his side and every part of his body rigid, he rocked from side to side with his knees locked to inch forward like some kind of malevolent penguin. After resuming normal posture, Pakomio explained that this was what the expression meant – but who on earth, he asked, would want to move in such a manner?

Lipo and Hunt then turned their attention to those statues that had been broken and abandoned beside Love's network of U-shaped roads. The vast majority of broken and discarded statues were found on sections of road with a slight gradient. Those discovered on slightly downhill sections were found lying face down, while those abandoned on uphill sections were uniformly discovered

lying face up. This reinforced the Lipo–Hunt hypothesis that the statues were moved upright and were therefore at their most precarious on gradients. They also noticed striking dissimilarities between the statues in situ and those abandoned by the roadside, the latter presenting a decidedly more bulbous lower torso to such an extent that they were almost like a bowling pin in profile. It was further noted that the bases of all the abandoned statues were D-shaped – with the straight line of the D to the rear of the statue – and angled downwards towards the front. In short, they had a much lower centre of gravity than those in situ and were decidedly 'wobbly' on their feet, with the angle on the base inclining them to lean slightly forward when stood upright.

When their replica Mo'ai arrived in early 2012, Lipo and Hunt were ready to conduct their experiment.

Dividing their eighteen-strong workforce into three teams, Lipo and Hunt tied one rope about their statue's head and two others about its base so that two teams could twist the statue from side to side to make it 'walk' as the third team likewise rocked it to and fro on its base. After a few false starts and the repositioning of the ropes, they were off, successfully 'walking' their statue 100 metres along the concave rut in a swept section of road in forty minutes. Allowing for the proficiency of people experienced in such techniques, Lipo and Hunt reckoned that the islanders would have had no trouble in 'walking' one of their statues at least a kilometre a day. Once in position, the statue would have its base chipped level, its eyes completed and painted to bring it 'alive', and its torso slimmed to a more natural profile.

The Lipo–Hunt hypothesis drew praise from some sectors of archaeological academe and indignant howls from others – most notably those in the sledge-and-rollers lobby. It must be said that their hypothesis as to how the giant statues were moved is the only one to date that concurs with local oral tradition, and makes sense of the concave roads and the profile variance between those statues lying abandoned and those in situ. Besides, rollers made from the trunk of the palm tree, with its soft and spongy interior, would have 'squidged' and split under the weight, which brings us to the nature of the ecological disaster that overtook the island.

It was once thought that the islanders chopped down so many trees to make rollers for their statue obsession that they deforested their own habitat. But more diligent study of the island revealed that, when the first Polynesians stepped ashore, there would have been something like 20 million palm trees, which means that there would have been up to 20,000 trees available per statue. Not only is it unrealistic that they would have used so many trees per statue but, as mentioned previously, the spongy and pliable nature of the palm tree, which allows it to survive tropical storms, would hardly make for functional rollers on a concave road surface. With its population peaking at the 12,000 mark in the fifteenth century, the ecosystem of Easter Island was destroyed by factors other than the supposed use of palm trees for rollers: it was a concatenation of poor management of the available resources and the ravenous Polynesian rat. Factor in invading Europeans and South Americans with guns, disease and a hunger for slaves, and you have the perfect storm to reduce the population of Easter Island to 111 by 1877.

As a farming people with no use for palm trees, the Polynesian settlers opted for an aggressive slash-and-burn policy when it came to land clearance – they also munched their way through the entire population of land- and seabirds, which provided the guano so essential to the health and propagation of those trees that remained. And then there were the rats that were unwittingly brought to the island on rafts and other crafts. With their numbers unchecked by the presence of natural predators and encouraged by an abundant food source, as was the case on Easter Island, even a single pair of rats can produce a population of many millions within three years – and the rats' preferred snack was the seeds of the palm tree. Between them, the humans and the rats wiped out all the trees to leave the island vulnerable to wind and rain

THE SHUFFLE

Although they were the first to identify the specific mechanics required to make the statues 'walk', archaeologists Carl Lipo and Terry Hunt were not the first to realize that they might have been 'shuffled' along to move them into position. This was first proposed by the French anthropologist Jean-Michel Schwartz in his book *The Mysteries of Easter Island* (1975).

Schwartz's suggestion inspired Pavel Pavel, a Czech engineer with an interest in how ancient cultures moved heavy weights, to make his own replica Mo'ai in 1982 and try to make it 'walk'. In 1986, Thor Heyerdahl invited Pavel to accompany him to Easter Island and try out his ideas with real Mo'ais.

Most of their efforts involved rocking a Mo'ai from side to side using two small teams while a third team yanked rhythmically on a rope to drag the statue forward. While they did enjoy some limited success, they achieved nothing like the ease of movement later established by Lipo and Hunt with their method of twisting the base of the Mo'ai while it was rocked to and fro.

erosion, and general degradation. In the times of hardship thus brought upon their own heads, the islanders then fell into civil war – or so the story goes.

This aspect of the island's history was first brought to European ears by the Norwegian explorer Thor Heyerdahl, best known for his 1947 *Kon-Tiki* expedition to the Polynesian islands. Allegedly there were two distinct groups or social classes on Easter Island – the Long-eared people thought themselves a cut above the Short-eared people, and kept them in a state of slavery from which they rebelled to slaughter their oppressors. But the Western perception of this legend is slightly skewed by the mistranslation of the designation *Hanau Eepe*, which, properly translated as the short and stocky people, was confused with the Rapa Nuian '*epe*', meaning ear – so the fictitious battle was not between Long- and Short-eared peoples but between those who were short and fat and those who were tall and thin.

No one knows why, but the arrival of the first Dutch explorers in 1722 brought about an immediate cessation in statue production. Perhaps their positioning about the island's shoreline was intended to ward off invaders and, as they had failed in this supposed duty, the statues forfeited the islanders' respect; if the ancestors have abandoned us then why don't we abandon them, they might have reasoned. Either way, across the next hundred years or so, with successive incursions onto the island by Dutch, Spanish and British expeditions – not to mention Peruvian slavers – all the statues fell in what the islanders call the *Huri Mo'ai*, or the casting down of the statues. Some islanders say this desecration was deliberate, others attribute it to 'an angry shaking of the earth', but, whichever it was, most of the statues have now been re-erected by the 5,000 islanders, supported by the tourist trade.

———◄o►———

3

Murder Most Foul

CLEOPATRA'S COBRA:
THE DEATH OF THE LAST
QUEEN OF EGYPT

IT IS PROBABLY fair to say that if Sir Thomas North had not published his translation of Plutarch's *Parallel Lives* in 1579, which Shakespeare used as the foundation for his 1607 blockbuster, *Antony and Cleopatra*, then few today would be so familiar with either character and Cleopatra wouldn't be so misrepresented in popular culture. She is now condemned to being portrayed as the Egyptian vamp-of-the-Nile who used her seductive powers to ensnare the likes of Caesar and Mark Antony, but this frivolous image obscures the reality of a woman who was an intellectual powerhouse driven by a steely resolve. The most fascinating aspect of the complexity that was Cleopatra was between her ears – not her bedsheets.

The foundations of the dynasty to which Cleopatra belonged were laid by Ptolemy Lagides in 323 BC and destined to endure for over three centuries. He had been a sub-commander of Alexander the Great and possibly his half-brother, since Ptolemy's mother, Arsinoe, was a concubine of Philip II of Macedon. Either way, after Alexander's death and with his empire in a state of decline, Ptolemy, backed by an army of considerable size, marched into ancient Egypt to establish a Hellenistic realm of which he declared himself king. It was Ptolemy V who instituted 'Cleopatra' as a royal title based on the Greek for flame or glory of the father, and some fifteen queens or queens-in-waiting bore the title through the ages. The lady in question here was Cleopatra VII (69 to 30 BC), the daughter of Ptolemy XII whose name was Thea Philopator, again from the Greek and meaning the goddess who loves her father. As it turned out, she was also destined to be the last absolute ruler of ancient Egypt.

After the assassination of Julius Caesar, Cleopatra's main supporter, she arranged to meet with Mark Antony in Tarsus in Asia Minor and it was here in 41 BC that the pair began plotting their doomed venture to isolate Egypt from Roman control. Within four years they were in control in Egypt, with Mark Antony effectively declaring independence from Rome. Octavian, the future Emperor Augustus, came after them to seal the fate of both with his destruction of the Egyptian fleet at the Battle of Actium (31 BC), just off the coast of Greece. With Octavian in hot pursuit the pair fled but, once back in Egypt, Antony found his land forces had deserted him. When Octavian caught up with them in August of 30 BC, Antony was in hiding while Cleopatra remained in her palace. It is what happened next that has been shrouded in mystery – was she pushed or did she jump?

According to the Roman historian Plutarch, and later Cassius Dio, the fact that Cleopatra remained stubbornly alive and locked in her mausoleum presented Octavian with a quandary. There were pros and cons to killing her – but her blood could not be seen to be on Octavian's hands. One way or another, a note was delivered to Mark Antony by one of Cleopatra's servants telling him that she had committed suicide and that he might as well do likewise. It is unclear whether this note was sent openly by Octavian, by Octavian pretending to be Cleopatra or by Cleopatra herself. If the latter were true, then this would square with the accounts of preliminary negotiations between Octavian and Cleopatra, where she was promised (falsely) that there might be a way for her to remain on the Egyptian throne, but under much tighter control from Rome. For that to be discussed, however, she must first secure the death of Mark Antony. Either way, it worked; Mark Antony fell on his sword.

Thanks again to Plutarch and Dio, we know that Octavian had toyed with the idea of dragging Cleopatra through the streets of Rome in chains for his parade of triumph. He remembered all too well, however, that when Julius Caesar had done this to Cleopatra's half-sister, Arsinoe, it had backfired, as her fragile dignity had aroused such pity among the mob that their bays of disapproval drowned out the cheers. Aware of the value of popular support, Octavian was not about to risk such a PR gaffe. But what if Cleopatra thought that was to be her fate? Surely she would then 'do the decent thing' and kill herself. Either by accident or design, news of such a fate certainly reached Cleopatra's ears, at which point she seems to have decided that death was the preferable option.

THE LEGACY

Cleopatra had four children, the oldest being Caesarion, who was allegedly fathered by Julius Caesar, though he always denied paternity. Eleven days after her death, Octavian had Caesarion killed just in case he really was the son of Julius and thus a contender for the throne in Rome. Cleopatra also had two sons with Mark Antony – Alexander and Ptolemy Philadelphus – and a girl called Cleopatra Selene.

After Cleopatra's death, these children were taken back to Rome by Octavian and sent to live with his sister, Octavia, who was also the abandoned wife of Mark Antony. After this, the two boys disappeared from historical records, with the strong suggestion that Selene, keeping up the old family traditions, had them bumped off to clear the stage for herself.

In 26 BC Octavian, by then Emperor Augustus, gave Selene a massive dowry to marry King Juba of Numidia – modern Algeria – on the condition that they pledged allegiance to Rome and took up the joint rule of the Roman province of Mauritania which, under the canny hand of Selene, became the Kingdom of Morocco.

The notion that such oblivion was bestowed on her and her two handmaidens by an asp – the Egyptian cobra – is wholly untenable. She summoned a servant to carry a note to Octavian informing him of her decision and, with his apartments but a few minutes distant, he immediately ran over to her to find her in a serene, deathly state. The Egyptian cobra is rightly feared as its neurotoxic/necrotoxic venom induces serious swelling, bruising and blistering at the site of the bite before the onset of nausea, vomiting, diarrhoea, convulsions and flaccid paralysis. Death is neither pleasant nor swift, and victims can take anything from two to eight hours to die, writhing in agony rather than lying in serene repose, as Cleopatra was reported to have done. If she killed herself, it was likely by other means: every ruler of Cleopatra's day kept handy a swift-acting poison to take when the game was played out, and Cleopatra was no exception. She was known to have carried such a potion in a bodkin she kept woven into her wig. So how did the silly snake idea get started?

Happy to risk parading Cleopatra in effigy through Rome, Octavian made a statue of her reclining on a couch with an Egyptian cobra wrapped about her right biceps and its head across her breast. This was not meant to indicate the manner of her death, but rather was a symbol of the dynasty that Octavian had brought to heel – people just got the wrong idea. That said, once the idea of her death by cobra had taken root, Octavian and others did all they could to keep that bandwagon rolling. Cleopatra was enthusiastically painted as a vile witch who used black magic sex to enslave men and as a 'lascivious fury' who was 'the shame of Egypt'. The snake tale suited the portrait and was further embellished, with the creature having been smuggled into her apartments in a basket of figs. This was really just a bit of smutty innuendo. The sexual symbolism of the snake needs no explanation but in Rome the fig was an equally potent sexual symbol in its own right. The Roman equivalent of the two-fingered salute was the *fico*, or the fig, as made by the extension of the thumb between the first two fingers of the clenched fist. (Those who proclaim they 'could not give two figs' about something are waxing cruder than they think.)

So much for the death of Antony and Cleopatra – but where are the bodies buried? Octavian is recorded as having granted their wish to be entombed together but his records annoyingly neglect to say exactly where that tomb was located. Perhaps this was a deliberate omission on his part, not wanting their tomb to become a rallying point for some kind of revolution. If they were buried anywhere near the splendour that was her palace at Alexandria, the tomb is lost for ever as that now lies beneath the sea. Dr Zahi Hawass, a prominent if controversial Egyptian archaeologist who was until 2001 the Minister of Antiquities, is concentrating his search 30 miles inland at the ruins of the Temple of Osiris at Taposiris Magna. Here he has not only found a number of coins bearing the image of Cleopatra and others of Mark Antony, but all the mummies in the hidden chambers surrounding the temple have been interred with their heads turned to the Temple of Osiris, indicating that there is someone important therein.

SYPHILIS OR SALIERI: MOZART'S KILLER

THAT MOZART WAS a musical genius is probably beyond question. A child prodigy, he could write music before he could write his own name, with half of all his symphonies created between the ages of eight and nineteen. He was also something of a raving pervert with a scatological obsession bordering on the pathological; the contents of letters exchanged with his similarly inclined mother simply cannot be referenced or quoted here. Let's just say that the same mind that conjured forth 'Eine Kleine Nachtmusik' (A Little Night Music) also spawned his less-publicized 'Leck mich im Arsch' (Lick Me in the Arse), a canon in B-flat major, Mozart catalogue number K231. He also wrote a sequel to said ditty with a title best not here revealed. But was he killed by his allegedly envious rival, Antonio Salieri? This is a popular theory presented as fact in the highly acclaimed and much-awarded *Amadeus* (1984), the film from which present generations have gleaned their perception of the whole Mozart–Salieri saga.

In that film and in accordance with the popular perception of Mozart and Salieri, the former is played by a youthful Tom Hulce and the latter by the older F. Murray Abraham, who gives a performance as the older burnout with the cocky young genius snapping at his heels. In reality they were of similar age – Mozart was born 1756 and Salieri in 1750 – with the latter at the time of their meeting in Vienna secure in his position as Kapellmeister of the city and very much at the top of his game. The only musical rivalry in the city was a very broad-fronted one between the German faction and the Italian; there is no evidence of acute points of personal animosity and certainly none between Mozart and Salieri, each the leading light of their own respective factions.

Never in the best of physical health – Mozart had possibly already suffered the ravages of syphilis, typhoid, smallpox, bronchitis, pneumonia and three bouts of rheumatic fever – he went into a sudden and rapid decline in November 1791, aged just thirty-five. According to all eyewitnesses, his condition was marked by high fever, nausea, double incontinence and pronounced sweating, and the stench of putrefaction permeated his room. Within two weeks his entire body resembled a bloated mass, and he lapsed into a coma before dying. True, at the onset of this condition he had himself started the poisoning rumour by rambling on to his wife, Constanze, that someone from the Italian faction must have slipped him a dose of Aqua Tofana, a colourless, tasteless yet quite lethal blend of arsenic, lead and belladonna that was indistinguishable from water. Supposedly invented in the early seventeenth century by one Guilia Tofana of Palermo in Italy and still accepted as a reality by many, such an insidious poison was pure fiction. The preeminent A. C. Grayling, Master of the New College of Humanities in London, addressed the

subject in his *The Heart of Things* (2006), asserting Aqua Tofana to have been an urban myth used to frighten and titillate courts across Europe. Had such a poison existed and been given to Mozart, then he would not have had a chance to say anything to anyone.

Even sticking with standard arsenic, had a single and lethal dose been administered Mozart would have been dead within hours or, at best, a couple of days. Incremental doses were favoured by some poisoners but this required continual access to the victim. Yet the only people with Mozart throughout his well-documented decline were members of his immediate family and his physician Dr Nikolaus Closset. As the symptoms suffered by Mozart fail to match those of arsenic poisoning, some have speculated that he was just another victim of a highly aggressive streptococcal infection that was doing the rounds of the city at the time. An alternative theory, advanced in 2001 by Professor Jan Hirschmann of the School of Medicine at the University of Washington and considered likely by many, maintains the culprit to have been trichinosis, an infection contracted from eating (contaminated) pork, a meat of which Mozart was inordinately fond. Ingestion of the parasitic trichinella worm, which so often infests pork meat and can survive inadequate cooking, does indeed induce symptoms similar to those endured by Mozart. Retrospective diagnosis is hardly an exact science and more useful in the elimination of causes of death than it is in causal identification, but Hirschmann's paper is of particular interest as it goes to great lengths to explain why neither arsenic nor any other poison of the time could possibly have been involved.

Also enshrined in popular myth is the image of a penniless Mozart being buried in a pauper's grave during a blizzard with few in attendance. Mozart was buried in the manner prescribed for all by the burial regulations for Vienna as decreed in 1784 by the Emperor Joseph: due to a lack of space, it was decided that all – except, of course, the elite – should be buried in a grave which would be reopened every ten years so the remains could be cleared and the grave reused. His funeral was organized by Baron Gottfried van Swieten and attended by many, including Salieri and other musical notables. All the blizzard nonsense was dreamed up by a journalist called Joseph Deiner who, falsely claiming attendance, wrote an article in the Vienna *Morgen-Post* of 28 January 1856, telling of the pitifully small band of mourners bent against the raging blizzard, which eventually drove them from the grave. The records of the Vienna Observatory, on the other hand, notes the weather on 6 December 1791 to have been 'mild with frequent mist; temperatures ranging from 37°F–38°F with a weak east wind throughout the day'.

THE MOZART LEGACY

Although known as Wolfgang Amadeus Mozart, the composer was christened Johannes Chrysostomus Wolfgangus Theophilus Mozart, a cumbersome mouthful, which is likely the reason he was known to his wife and intimates as Wolferl.

Although he and Constanze had six children, only two survived infancy; Karl Thomas, who died in 1858, and Franz Xaver, who died in 1844, with neither of them ever marrying or fathering a child. Franz enjoyed some limited success as a composer-conductor while Karl spent most of his life in clerical jobs after going bankrupt with a piano store in Livorno. When he died, so too did the direct Mozart line.

That said, the indirect Mozart line did make it into the twentieth century with Bertha Forschter, the great-granddaughter of Mozart's sister, Maria Anna, dying in 1917, while Karoline Grau, the great-great-grandniece of Mozart's father, Leopold, only passed away in 1965.

After the funeral, word of Mozart's paranoid ramblings about poison leaked out to be whipped into a maelstrom of gossip around Vienna. As the unofficial head of the Italian faction, Salieri was taunted by whispers that he killed the young genius out of spite and envy. Mozart's wife, Constanze, infuriatingly portrayed as a vacuous airhead in so many biopics, certainly placed no credence in such gossip as, a few years after her husband's death, she sent their son Franz to Salieri for tutoring, something she would hardly do if she thought the man had murdered her husband. Multilingual and no mean soprano herself, it was Constanze who, after Mozart's death, organized memorial concerts across Europe and became the diligent custodian of his catalogue of compositions to ensure her husband's death would only be the beginning of his fame.

As for Salieri, the spiteful gossip branding him a murderer weighed heavy on his mind as the hushed sniggers dogged the footsteps of his career. Hospitalized with dementia in 1823, in his darker moments he could be found wandering and deranged, screaming that he was the man who killed Mozart. In 1830, Pushkin penned a melodrama called *Mozart and Salieri*, which unequivocally branded Salieri as the machinating murderer, with Rimsky-Korsakov transforming that play into the libretto for his 1897 opera of the same name. In 1979, Peter Shaffer used the Pushkin original as the foundation for his play *Amadeus* which, to bring us full circle, was made into the film from which most take their impression of the two protagonists.

But the mysteries surrounding Mozart don't end there – what happened to his skull? One story goes that when officiating at Mozart's burial, Joseph Rothmayr, the sexton at St Marx Cemetery, twisted a length of wire about the corpse's neck to facilitate later identification and, when officiating at the exhumation of that same communal grave a decade later, he stole the skull as a keepsake. When he retired, Rothmayr left his gruesome trophy to his successor, Joseph Radshopf who, in 1842, passed it on to a Viennese engraver called Jakob Hyrtl. Finding the skull 'staring' at him across his desk a trifle unsettling, Hyrtl gave it to his brother, Joseph, the chair of anatomy at the University of Vienna, who had an interest in the now-discredited 'science' of phrenology and thus his own considerable collection of skulls. Having once refused to sell the skull to Mozart's hometown of Salzburg, despite a princely offer of 200 silver thalers, Hyrtl's family donated it to the International Mozarteum Foundation in that city. But the mystery was not yet over.

In 2006 the Austrian Broadcasting Corporation, known domestically as ORF, hired a team of geneticists to determine whether the skull held by the Mozarteum was indeed that of the long-dead composer. Taking DNA material from the remains of his niece, Jeanette, and his maternal grandmother, Eva Rosine Pertl, exhumed at Salzburg's St Sebastian Cemetery, comparison tests were run against material extracted from teeth in the skull. But, to everyone's astonishment, no genetic link could be established between any two of the three samples. If the rest of Mozart's kin were as promiscuous as he was, then rampant illegitimacy throughout such a family would come as no surprise; either that, or the skull held by the Mozarteum is not that of the composer. In the musical circles of both Vienna and Salzburg there is a wry maxim stating that there may be a dozen Mozart skulls in existence, but only three of them are genuine.

◄○►

THE PEASANT WHO KNEW
TOO MUCH: THE DEATH
OF RASPUTIN

BORN IN 1869, Grigori Rasputin was a charismatic and Machiavellian machinator popularly believed to have been able to control the Tsarevich's haemophilia by hypnosis. By 1905, this placed Rasputin in the Russian Tsar's inner circle, a position he abused by using that same hypnotic power allegedly to seduce the Tsarina, a scandal which led to his death at the hands of Russian nobility. Likewise, the nightmarish account of that assassination has provided the content of many a film in which the dishevelled mystic is poisoned, repeatedly shot and stabbed, and hit with everything but the kitchen sink, yet is still alive when he is rolled up in a carpet and dumped in the freezing Neva river. All such melodrama appears to be lurid invention; indications are that in fact Rasputin was assassinated in 1916 by the British Secret Intelligence Service (SIS). But how did such a malodorous peasant insinuate himself into the upper echelons of the grandest royal court of the day?

The Russian royal court of Nicholas II and Alexandra was opulent beyond imagination but much of the country was locked in a sort of medieval culture long abandoned by the rest of Europe, with serfdom not completely abolished until 1892. Many at court were obsessed with the occult and constantly on the search for the next prophet to act as their hotline to God. Nicholas certainly believed that God spoke through the mouths of simpletons and the demented, prompting him to welcome into his court a succession of lunatics – and charlatans acting the part – to be consulted on matters of domestic or foreign policy. In 1903 Eric Weiss, aka Harry Houdini, was invited to perform for the court. Nicholas went into raptures and, ignoring Houdini's insistence that all was smoke and mirrors, proclaimed him to the court to be the genuine *Volshebnik* (Wizard or Miracle Man) for whom they had all been waiting. Politely turning down the Tsar's pleadings for him to remain at court in such a capacity and later explaining his very real fears that the court might hold him captive, like some performing animal, Houdini fled the city just as Rasputin arrived in St Petersburg to find the stage set and the role of *Volshebnik* open for the taking.

Having heard of Rasputin's alleged healing powers, Alexandra sent for him to see if he could do anything about her son's haemophilia. He did seem to have a positive effect on reducing the severity of the distressing bouts of both internal and external bleeding. Some have suggested that he used hypnosis to calm the boy and slow down his heart rate but there is no evidence that Rasputin was skilled in Mesmer's art. More likely, his intervention kept at bay the court doctors with their leeches, coupled with their use of a new wonder drug called aspirin, now recognized as an

extraordinarily efficient anti-clotting agent, so not the best treatment for a haemophiliac. Something about Rasputin's presence seemed to work for the child so the Tsar and Tsarina were from then on in thrall to him.

To keep the royals compliant, Rasputin encouraged their experimental drug-taking until Alexandra was hopelessly addicted to barbiturates, cocaine and morphine while Nicholas was endlessly puffing on marijuana joints laced with psychotropic henbane. Now believing himself to be in a position to influence foreign policy, Rasputin started to pressure the Tsar into withdrawing from the First World War. But this was to prove his undoing. Well aware of the extent of Rasputin's influence over the Tsar, alarm bells started ringing in the British Secret Intelligence Service, which also suspected, quite rightly, that he had opened up lines of communication to German intelligence by presenting himself as a peace broker. Russia's withdrawal from the war would result in 350,000 German troops making a U-turn for the Western Front where such numbers would tip the balance in favour of Berlin. Rasputin had to go.

With the machinations of a secret service being, by their very nature, secret, we will never be sure of the details but the following is what most consider to be the likely chain of events leading up to the death of Rasputin. Towards the close of 1916, Captain Oswald Rayner of the SIS was ordered to re-establish contact with his one-time lover, Prince Felix Yusupov; the pair had studied together at Oxford and Yusupov, a flamboyant transvestite, was but one of many courtiers anxious to be rid of Rasputin. Already based in Petrograd (as St Petersburg was named from the beginning of the First World War), Rayner, his deputy Stephen Alley (who had been born at the Yusupov palace as his father had been a tutor to the young Felix) and another SIS officer called John Scale, started to lay their plans. Rayner contacted Yusupov and the pair met frequently in the days leading up to the assassination; this is borne out by the log of Rayner's driver, which details the visits to the Yusupov Moika Palace, the penultimate visit on the day before the killing and the last the day after. It was agreed that Yusupov would lure Rasputin to the Moika on 30 December 1916 (17 December on the Old Style Russian calendar then in use) with the promise of a night of drunken debauchery. After a fairly brutal struggle involving Yusupov and a couple of other Russian nobles, during which Rasputin took a hit from a small-calibre bullet, Rayner stepped in and shot Rasputin point-blank in the middle of the forehead with his Webley .445 service revolver. No slavering demon refusing to die: down he went like a sack of potatoes. As the Russian contingent struggled to compose themselves, Rayner and associates trussed up the body, rolled it up in a carpet and, under cover of dark, dumped it in the nearby freezing river.

But it is, of course, Yusupov's nightmarish account of the event which, delivered up for public consumption, was designed to obscure the fact that he had involved the agents of a foreign power in Russian internal affairs. It also made him look like the saviour of Mother Russia, ridding the country of a man seen by many as the devil incarnate. He claimed that in preparation for Rasputin's visit he had laced all the miniature cakes and Madeira with copious amounts of cyanide but that his demonic visitor simply scoffed and swigged away like there was no tomorrow. So, he shot Rasputin twice through the heart at close range but this only made him angry. Now allegedly joined by the other nobles, the group collectively shot their victim a few more times, stabbed him, kicked him in the head and stamped on his throat. Yet when they left him for dead and returned with the carpet, Rasputin leapt up to attack them, which called for more shooting, stabbing, clubbing, etc., before they carried out the still-snarling Rasputin to drown him in the river.

THE REAL RASPUTIN

Born Grigori Yefimovich Novykh in Siberia in 1869, Rasputin was a troublesome teenager, much involved in anti-social behaviour and petty crime. In 1887 he was married to Praskovya Dubrovina, with whom he had seven children before having to go on the run in 1897 for horse rustling, but his abandoned wife remained devoted to Grigori to the end. Only three of their children, Maria, Dimitri and Vavara, survived into adulthood.

Once on the road, Grigori realized the profits to be had from becoming a peripatetic mystic and adopted the epithet of Rasputin, which means 'the debauchee', before coming up with the concept of salvation through sin. Needless to say, he had little trouble in attracting neophytes to that doctrinal banner.

By 1905 he was working his charms in St Petersburg, where he managed to enthral the Princesses Militsa and Anastasia of Montenegro, both married to cousins of the Tsar – and the rest, as they say, is history.

The first problem with the Yusupov account centres on his mention of Madeira wine and the petit-fours, both of which would have been agonizing for Rasputin to consume. On 29 June 1914 he had been attacked by a peasant woman called Khioniya Guseva who, after slicing open his abdomen, ran through the streets shrieking that she had killed the Anti-Christ. The damage left Rasputin with hyper-acidosis, making the ingestion of any sugar an extremely painful experience. Furthermore, the original autopsy performed by Professor Dmitry Kossorotov found no trace of poison in the body – and he was actively seeking it after hearing the Yusupov account – and the lungs contained no water, leaving cause of death to be a single shot to the forehead from a heavy-calibre pistol. This autopsy was reviewed in 1993 by Dr Vladimir Zharov and again in 2005 by the pre-eminent forensic pathologist Dr Derrick Pounder, with neither finding any fault with the original. Also involved in that review of 2005 was the Firearms Department of the Imperial War Museum, which, after studying the forensic photographs taken of Rasputin's head at the time, commented that 'the size and prominence of the abraded margin of the entry-point [of the kill-shot] indicated a large lead and unjacketed bullet', which they suggested came from a Webley .445 British officer's pistol. At the time, Britain was unique in that its service pistols still used the old-style unjacketed and heavy lead slug.

Fearing for her own life, Rasputin's daughter, Maria, fled first to Bucharest to work as an 'exotic' dancer and then to the United States where she toured with Ringling Bros Circus as a lion tamer. The Yusupovs, too, ended up in the States where they sued MGM over *Rasputin and the Empress* (1932), a film which falsely depicted Irina Yusupov, thinly disguised as the Princess Natasha, as one of Rasputin's sexual conquests. MGM had to stump up a large settlement plus costs, which prompted all film producers thenceforth to add the now familiar disclaimer stating that: 'any similarity to persons living or dead is purely coincidental', etc.

As for Rasputin himself, he would prove more trouble dead than alive. In 1917 the Germans, still furious at the British for bumping off the man most likely to drag Russia out of the war, turned their attentions to Lenin, then sulking in exile in Switzerland, and to Trotsky, who languished in New York. Having filled the latter's pockets with gold and sent him back to Russia, they also put Lenin on a sealed train with 50 million gold marks and likewise returned him to Russia to take control of the chaos and keep Russia far too busy with internal upheaval to be bothered with any war in Europe. And it was money well spent; Russia did withdraw from the First World War as the result of the capitalist-funded Communist revolution.

———◄o►———

THE BODY IN THE BASEMENT: THE MISTRIAL OF DR CRIPPEN

THE ENDURING PROMINENCE of Dr Hawley Harvey Crippen in the annals of British crime – second only to that of Jack the Ripper – is itself a mystery. At most, he only killed one person, while there were other more prolific killers from his era who few today could name. And it now seems that the human remains found in the basement of his home at 39 Hilldrop Crescent in the London district of Holloway were in fact not those of his wife, for whose murder he was hanged in 1910.

The title of 'doctor' is stretching things a bit as Crippen only studied homeopathy for a short while in 1884 before 'graduating' from the Cleveland Homeopathy Medical College. Moving to New York to set up a practice in 1894, he met and married Kunigunde Mackamotski, also known as Cora, a woman of unrealistic theatrical ambition and a voracious sexual appetite who quickly recognized the diminutive and mousey Crippen as a compliant meal-ticket she could wrap around her little finger. Determined to advance her career, she badgered Crippen into moving to London where, with his rather meaningless qualifications wholly unrecognized, he was left with no option but to take work as a distributor of patented medicines. By 1905 the couple were in residence at Hilldrop Crescent where they were obliged to take in lodgers to supplement Crippen's meagre earnings, providing Cora with a string of lovers. In 1908, Crippen took the much younger Ethel Neave, who liked to be known as Ethel Le Neve, as his own lover. After a house party on 31 January 1910, Cora disappeared, her absence explained by Crippen as her having returned to the United States where she had died suddenly in California.

Their suspicions aroused by Neave moving into Hilldrop Crescent and disporting herself in Cora's clothes and jewellery, the missing wife's friends made representations to the police who, in the form of Inspector Dew of Scotland Yard, paid Crippen a visit. He was told that the story was in fact a lie invented to cover the shame of Cora having run away to the States with an actor called Bruce Miller. After a cursory search of the house the police left. Worried by the visit, the couple, fearing arrest for a murder they had not in fact committed, fled to Antwerp to board the SS *Montrose*, bound for Canada, under the name of Robinson, father and son, with Ethel disguised as a boy. Their disappearance from London prompted further and more diligent searches of Hilldrop Crescent and, this time, human remains were found under the brick floor of the basement. After a cable from the captain of the *Montrose*, by now very suspicious of the 'boy' Robinson, Dew boarded the faster SS *Laurentic* so he would reach Canada in time to arrest the pair as their ship docked.

Crippen was brought back to England and his trial began at the Old Bailey on 18 October 1910 with Bernard Spilsbury, pathologist and proto-forensic scientist, as the star witness for the prosecution. Of limited academic qualifications himself, Spilsbury was nevertheless a handsome and charismatic man with an imposing courtroom presence and an ability to assert his opinions with such authority that few dared challenge him. Indeed, it was said at the time that he only had to show his face in court for it to bode ill for any defendant. In his matter-of-fact way, Spilsbury asserted that the remains were those of Cora Crippen as a still-visible scar on one of the tissue samples matched her medical records, which listed an appendectomy. He further asserted that the remains showed high levels of hyoscine, a preparation Crippen is listed as having purchased shortly before Cora's disappearance, and that curlers containing hair consistent with hers were also found with the remains, as was the cord from a pair of pyjamas found in Crippen's bedroom. The brand of these pyjamas was not available on the UK market prior to 1908 and thus within the relevant timeframe. All very damning, to be sure. After Spilsbury had finished with them the jury retired for a mere twenty-seven minutes before returning with a guilty verdict, which resulted in Crippen hanging on 23 November. He was later buried within the confines of London's Pentonville Prison.

Later examination of the seemingly damning evidence casts serious doubt on Crippen's guilt. The hyoscine flagged by Spilsbury was in fact widely used for gastro-intestinal ailments and to be found in most homes.

SPILSBURY EXPOSED

By the 1920s cracks were appearing in Spilsbury's celebrity facade, with many questioning the 'spin' he imparted to his forensic evidence to help secure guilty verdicts and his insistence on working alone behind locked mortuary doors.

In 1923, Spilsbury's dogmatic evidence secured a guilty verdict against Corporal Albert Dearnley, accused of the murder of Corporal James Ellis. After a scant twenty-nine-minute jury deliberation, Spilsbury conclusively 'proved' Dearnley had bound and gagged his victim with the murderous intent required to ensure death by suffocation.

Actually, the two were lovers engaged in bondage suffocation games, a fact known to Spilsbury before he took the stand but one he suppressed due to his pronounced homophobia and reluctance to cause a scandal by revealing such practice in the armed forces. But the suppressed evidence was made public in time to save Dearnley from the rope, with Spilsbury dispassionately opining that he should have hanged anyway for being gay. In 1947, by which time his private life and reputation were in tatters, Spilsbury gassed himself in his laboratory at University College London.

And the pyjama cord is thought to have been planted by the beleaguered police, under a great deal of pressure to bring Crippen to book. On top of that, a letter, ostensibly from Cora in America, which taunted Crippen by saying that she had no intention of extricating him from his predicament by revealing her whereabouts, was 'buried' by the prosecution and never revealed to the defence during the trial. It would also later transpire that Spilsbury's dogmatic assertions, which sent Crippen and many others to the gallows, were quite untenable or even deliberately 'fudged' to keep himself in the prosecutorial limelight or, even worse, because he had taken a personal dislike to the defendant.

Even at the time, others were puzzled. Spilsbury, obviously forgetting that Dr Crippen was not in fact a doctor of any kind, had also made much of the fact that the remains showed signs of having been dissected by someone with proficient surgical skills. There is also a question mark over why he would poison her and then chop her up; surely the claim of an accidentally self-administered overdose of hyoscine would have been the way to go? And, having successfully disposed of the head, the limbs and some of the torso, why bury what was left under the basement floor and in quicklime which, when as wet as it was in the basement, preserves human remains – something that Crippen would have known?

Bringing more modern forensic techniques to bear on the extant evidence, in 2007 David Foran PhD, Professor and Director of the Forensic Science Programme at

Michigan State University, teamed up with American genealogist Beth Wills, who tracked down Cora's living female descendants. Working with three of Cora's great-nieces, it was established that neither the hair nor the remains were those of Cora Crippen and the 'scar' on the skin sample was just a fold in the skin – it still showed the presence of hair follicles, which are never found in scar tissue. Furthermore, the Y chromosome found in the tissue indicated beyond any doubt that the remains were those of a man, so why were curlers found with the remains? Most importantly, these revelations make the likelihood of the police having connived to 'sweeten' the pot of evidence against Crippen look more like a racing certainty.

So, if not Cora Crippen, then whose remains were disposed of in the basement of 39 Hilldrop Crescent? As Crippen and his defence had asserted all along, they must have been put there by some previous occupant of the house. Had he and Ethel just stayed put after the initial police visit to Hilldrop Crescent then it is likely that no further investigation would have taken place. As for Ethel, she of course fared better. Found not guilty of any involvement in the 'murder' of Cora, who in all likelihood had indeed decamped to the United States, she slipped into respectable obscurity. After the trial she hid in Canada and the States for a few years before returning to London to find work as a typist at Hampton's Furniture Store near Trafalgar Square. There she met and married a clerk called Stanley Smith to settle in Croydon and raise two children. Aged eighty-four, she died in 1967 with none of her new family knowing anything of her infamous past.

———◆◆———

ABANDONED TO THEIR FATE: ROMANOVS AND REVOLUTION

On 15 July 1891, the thirteen-year-old Yakov Yurovsky was part of the crowd lining the main street of Tomsk, one of the oldest settlements in Siberia, to welcome the visiting twenty-three-year-old Prince Nicholas, oldest son of the House of Romanov, Russia's royal family. 'I remember how handsome he was, with his neat brown beard; as he drew level he nodded and waved back at me,' Yurovsky recalled. In 1918, Yurovsky would be responsible for murdering Nicholas and his family.

By 1897, Yurovsky was a dedicated Communist revolutionary and the hardline agitator who organized Tomsk's first general labour strike, a short-lived fiasco for which he was banished from the city. Casting his lot to fate, Yurovsky closed his eyes and stuck a pin in a map to choose his new home, landing on Yekaterinburg, a city in the eastern Urals. By coincidence, this would also be the city in which the revolutionary Russian Red Army would soon be holding Tsar Nicholas and the Romanov family captive in the Ipatiev House, a deserted mansion they grimly code-named the 'House of Special Purpose'.

At about the same time as Yurovsky was being appointed Yekaterinburg's local commissar in 1917, Vladimir Lenin was being returned to Russia by the Germans to take control of the Red Revolution. The pro-Romanov White Army was still a viable force and, in the summer of 1918, was advancing on Yekaterinburg. The prospect of the Whites releasing the Romanovs to serve as figureheads for a counter-revolution was unthinkable; they had to die. Knowing this day would come sooner or later, Lenin had already identified Yurovsky as the perfect assassin; not only was he Red through and through but the troops under his command were Hungarian mercenaries and thus far less likely than any Russian contingent to turn squeamish over gunning down the Russian royal family. Besides, Lenin reasoned, if there was a domestic or international uproar over the killings he could always blame it on a bunch of foreigners over whom he had no control.

Taking charge of the Ipatiev House, Yurovsky told the Romanovs they were to be moved further from the fighting and that they should make ready but, when they presented themselves for transport on the night of 16–17 July 1918, they were met by a hail of gunfire. Yurovsky's unsettlingly detailed report makes for grim reading, especially the account of the deaths of the princesses who, despite being shot several times, seemed unscathed. It transpired they had so much gold wire wound about their bodies and so many jewels sewn into their dresses that they were virtually bulletproof, and eventually bayonets had to be rammed through their eye sockets. But why did it have to come to that? Why did George V refuse his cousin and family sanctuary in the United Kingdom?

Before the Bolsheviks and the Red Army had secured total power, quite a few countries had been approached as possible refuges but only Britain, initially, agreed. Although Labour Prime Minister David Lloyd George openly applauded the upheaval in Russia he assumed, wrongly as it turned out, that his king, George V, as cousin and close friend of the Tsar, would be happy for the family to be offered sanctuary. But George, or rather his Queen Consort, Mary, put her foot down. Gore Vidal, a close friend of both Princess Margaret and the Duke of Windsor, the abdicated Edward VIII, recalled in his memoirs a conversation he had with the latter in 1952 at the Capri villa of the Countess Mona von Bismarck. Vidal was informed by the Duke that when breakfasting with his parents the morning after Lloyd George had, off his own bat, offered to send a British warship to collect the Romanovs, an aide interrupted them with a note asking royal approval for the venture. George read it before passing it to Mary who uttered a most emphatic 'No.' This was repeated by George as he handed the note back to the aide for him to take the reply to the Prime Minister.

Mary's reasons for her blunt refusal of sanctuary focused on the fact that the Easter Rising in Ireland was still fresh in everybody's minds and that socialism, with its star on the rise in Britain, might be further stirred up by the Crown giving house room to the last of the autocrats and his family, who were proving such a thorn in the side of the great socialist uprising in Russia. Could this not trigger revolution in the UK? But there may have been other, more petty reasons, at the heart of Mary's decision to reject the Romanovs. Of lower station than others in the British and international royal elite and disliked by the British people for her German accent, Mary of Teck had long carried a chip on her shoulder, especially for Alexandra, Empress of Russia, who, rightly or wrongly, she felt sure took delight in slighting and demeaning her. To be fair, at the time of Mary's high-handed rejection of her own prime minister's proposed rescue venture, the Romanovs were simply confined to the palace at Tsarskoe

THE ROMANOVS

Nicholas and Alexandra Romanov were the authors of their own downfall. Neither were terribly bright, and the calamitous ineptitude of their rule was little improved by their addictions to barbiturates, opium and cocaine, nor by their obsession with the occult, which brought them under the malevolent control of Rasputin, a man seen by many as a religious charlatan with dangerous influence over the Tsar and his family. During the First World War, Tsar Nicholas II assumed control of the Russian Army, a move welcomed only by the Germans, relieved that command had not been delegated to generals who actually knew what they were doing. His absence left his wife Alexandra to run the country into the ground; when the people rioted in starvation she unleashed brigades of Cossack cavalry, which did nothing to improve her standing with the people. The Cossacks, however, mutinied to join those they were meant to attack, heralding the end of the Romanov dynasty as other military units followed the Cossack lead to fuel the Russian Revolution. In March 1917, Nicholas was forced to abdicate, bringing three centuries of Romanov rule to an end.

Selo by the interim Kerensky government. The Bolsheviks were not yet in power so none could have then imagined what was to befall them – but Mary's spite, if indeed that's what it was, certainly nudged the Romanovs a lot closer to Lenin's House of Special Purpose.

Shortly after, George seems to have changed his mind and asked Lloyd George to reinstate his offer to extract the Romanovs, but by that time the Prime Minister had himself executed a volte-face on the matter. He was by then openly praising the Russian revolutionaries in parliament and trying to cement close relationships with the new Russian leaders; it no longer seemed sensible to offer refuge to the Romanovs. Once branded a 'dangerous revolutionary socialist' by Edward VII, Lloyd George's initial enthusiasm to bring the Romanovs to Britain seems to have darkly mirrored the initial stance of George and Mary in that he too thought their presence might bring about a socialist revolution in the UK which, unlike the royal couple, he would have gleefully welcomed. Besides, he argued, with the Bolsheviks by then in undisputed power, the sending of a British warship into their territorial waters was out of the question. So, the Romanovs were abandoned to their fate.

———◁○▷———

THE DREYFUS AFFAIR:
THE ORIGINS OF THE
TOUR DE FRANCE

In September 1894, a French spy, embedded at the German Embassy in Paris as a cleaner, found in a wastepaper basket a handwritten note from an anonymous French Army officer offering to sell the Germans details of the new French artillery. Although roughly torn up, the note was easily reconstructed and in the following month all suspicion was focused on Alfred Dreyfus, a captain of artillery whose handwriting bore a passing similarity to that on the note. Dreyfus was not a popular man; despite his undoubtedly high intellect he was stand-offish and magnificently boring; worse still, his family hailed from Alsace, which was then part of Germany.

In a hurriedly arranged court martial, no evidence of substance was presented and the graphologist refuting the handwriting to be that of Dreyfus was virtually thrown out on his ear. The defendant was found guilty and packed off to Devil's Island, a penal colony off the coast of French Guiana. Fortunately for Dreyfus, it was named for the treacherous currents in the shark-infested waters about its shores rather than for anything diabolical that happened there. Although life on the other French prison islands was nothing short of hell, the political-category inmates of Devil's Island enjoyed comparative comfort. Measuring about three-quarters of a mile by less than a third of a mile and comprising about thirty acres, over half of which was quite uninhabitable, the island never held more than thirteen politically sensitive prisoners at any one time. Each prisoner had their own hut, was allowed to grow vegetables, could send and receive mail, and was given regular medical check-ups. But to the innocent captive a prison of any kind is still a prison and back in France the Dreyfus Affair was turning ugly.

With the political left and right so sharply divided by the affair in France, there were running battles in the boulevards and parks between the pro- and anti-Dreyfusards. In 1899, both the car-maker Comte de Dion and tyre magnate Édouard Michelin were arrested at the Auteuil racetrack for starting a ruckus during which Émile Loubet, the President of France, was whacked over the head with a walking stick. Actually, Loubet had not long been in power, having succeeded Félix Faure who, on 16 February 1899, had died in such highly unusual circumstances that many suspected he had become a victim of a pro-Dreyfusard plot. Attended that day at the Élysée Palace by his young mistress, Marguerite Steinheil, he allegedly died of a stroke as she performed on him what is perhaps best described here as 'the love that *cannot* speak its name'. But, with Faure an acknowledged anti-Semite and a man determined to keep Dreyfus exactly where he

was, it was strongly suspected that Steinheil, with links to the pro-Dreyfusard lobby, might have popped something into his drink to simulate a heart attack and then dropped his trousers to claim it was all due to his getting overexcited.

In August 1896, Major Ferdinand Esterhazy, the real traitor who offered information to the Germans, was exposed after correspondence between him and Maximilian von Schwartzkoppen, the German military attaché in Paris, was discovered by Marie Georges Picquart of the French army's intelligence bureau. Instead of acting on this, the authorities packed Picquart off to obscure duties in Tunisia with orders to keep his mouth shut. He sent all his proof to Dreyfus's lawyers, which sparked a new round of rioting, but the military still refused to backtrack. Determined not to have the verdict against Dreyfus overturned, the French High Command held a court martial behind locked doors to find Esterhazy innocent and more rioting in the streets ensued. He was allowed to slip quietly away to England and settle in Hertfordshire's leafy Harpenden where he whiled away his time writing anti-Semitic trash until his death in 1923. The only positive result of Esterhazy's exposure was that it escalated factional hostilities to such a degree that President Loubet offered Dreyfus a pardon in 1899, this being a 'take it or leave it and stay on Devil's Island' deal which Dreyfus grabbed with both hands.

This left him a pardoned traitor instead of an innocent man, so little changed and, as those factional hostilities rumbled on, France's leading member of the literati, Émile Zola, would soon pay with his life for his support of Dreyfus. Returning to his Paris apartment at 21 Rue de Bruxelles after a break in the country with his wife in September 1902, the couple lit the bedroom fire before retiring for the night. By the morning he was dead and Alexandrine barely alive, both overcome with carbon-monoxide poisoning. The police conducted tests, relighting the fire and shutting caged rodents in the room, but all survived. It seemed that Zola's death was a tragic accident – but such findings did not sit well with everyone. Even the commissioner in charge of the case, Pierre Cornette, had his doubts but he was ordered to close the case as accidental death and, if he wanted to hang onto this job and pension, to keep his mouth shut. But in 1928, Zola's killer made his deathbed confession. Chimney and roof maintenance contractor Henri-Charles Buronfosse had, in the days before the Zolas' well-publicized return to Paris, been working on the conjoined roofs of the apartment blocks along Rue de Bruxelles and admitted to deliberately placing a mat over Zola's chimney the evening of the couple's return and to have then removed it early the next morning so as not to arouse suspicions. At the time of Zola's death, Buronfosse was a leading member of Paul Déroulède's League of Patriots – a sort of French National Front – even serving as Déroulède's personal bodyguard. He was also remembered by others as having made death threats after reading Zola's famous 'J'Accuse' article, his open condemnation of the Dreyfus cover-up.

In the aftermath of Zola's death, accusations were rife in the media. The pro- and anti-Dreyfusard lobbies were at the time identified by the sporting papers they bought; those in support of Dreyfus tended to buy Le Vélo while their enemies favoured L'Auto. With the former printed on cheap and gaudy green-tinted paper and the latter on yellow paper, these dailies taunted each other over Zola's death until, in the spring of the following year, the factions decided to do battle in a protracted bike race they called

J'ACCUSE!

Splashed across the front page of the left-wing newspaper *L'Aurore*, dated 13 January 1898, Émile Zola's open condemnation of the anti-Semitic persecution of Captain Dreyfus and general corrupt malpractice was aimed at President Félix Faure. Left untitled by Zola, it was the newspaper's editor, Georges Clemenceau, himself later prime minister of France, who came up with the snappy headline of 'J'Accuse!' – an expression which has itself entered the political rhetoric of many a nation.

Arrested on charges of sedition and put on trial for criminal libel the following month, Zola knew he was facing a long jail term, so he made a dash for the boat train at Paris's Gare du Nord to arrive at London's Victoria Station with nothing but the clothes in which he stood.

Staying in a series of cheap hotels and relying on the kindness of strangers and supporters, Zola spent several months in London's south-east district of Upper Norwood, not returning to Paris until June 1899, four months after the spectacular collapse of the Faure government.

the Tour de France. With *Le Vélo* and *L'Auto* in charge of the event, it was the colour of the newspapers that gave rise to the yellow jersey accorded the winner and the green jersey sported by the stage winner. Given the socio-political significance of the race, cycling in the right colours suddenly became a popular way of demonstrating one's stance on Dreyfus, and partisan cycling clubs blossomed across France.

As for Alfred Dreyfus, he was finally exonerated by a military commission convened on 12 July 1906. However, the old animosities were still afoot in June 1908 when he attended the ceremony to transfer Zola's remains from the cemetery at Montmartre to the Pantheon in Paris's Fifth District. Standing beside Zola's mistress, Jeanne Rozerot, who, along with her children by Zola, had been cordially invited by the widow, Dreyfus became the target of assassination. Pushing through the crowd while shouting anti-Semitic slogans, journalist Louis Grégori fired a couple of shots but only managed to hit Dreyfus in the arm. And, just to prove that right-wing lunacy was still prominent in France, his trial only lasted a matter of hours before Grégori, who had fired in front of hundreds of witnesses, was found not guilty on 11 September 1908 by a carefully selected judge and jury.

On 12 July 1935, twenty-nine years after his exoneration and to the exact hour of that deliberation, Dreyfus died peacefully in Paris before being laid to rest with military honours normally accorded those well above his then rank of lieutenant-colonel. His funeral cortege was allowed to pass through the ranks of officials and dignitaries assembled in the Place de la Concorde for the Bastille Day celebrations as it made its way to Montmartre cemetery, which was as close to an official apology as Dreyfus ever got.

————◇————

4

Riddles of Ritual and Religion

THE GREAT PYRAMID MYSTERY:
THE WHO, WHY AND HOW

ERECTED SOME 4,500 years ago outside Giza, a city still standing on the west bank of the Nile, it is no surprise that structures as impressive as the pyramids have provoked so much debate over how they were built and exactly who it was who laboured on their construction. The largest of the three, the 481-foot Great Pyramid commissioned by the Fourth Dynasty King Cheops, was for nearly 4,000 years the tallest manmade structure on the planet. The completion of Lincoln Cathedral in the first decade of the fourteenth century finally surpassed it when its main spire reached 520 feet above the ground, but the Great Pyramid reclaimed its title in 1549 when that usurper was blown down in a storm.

The Great Pyramid alone comprises something in the region of 2.3 million blocks of stone, the majority of which are limestone blocks weighing an average of 2.5 tons, but with several internal granite blocks, weighing anything from 15 tons to a staggering 70 tons. So, how did a pre-Iron Age people cut so many limestone blocks with such precision as to allow a tolerance of less than 2 mm, no matter how non-symmetrical the stones' respective interfaces? The only metal the Egyptians had at the time was copper, which is far too soft to perform such tasks. Next, we have the problem of how such stones were transported from the quarry and hauled up the sides of the ever-increasing pyramid-in-progress; the Egyptians had no pulleys or wheeled vehicles. They were certainly aware of the principle of the wheel as they had potters' wheels and irrigation wheels but even had they thought of using animal-drawn carts to move the stones they would have needed iron axles to take such weights; copper ones would have buckled or snapped at the first load.

The most popular theory about the method of construction maintains that the workforce must have been divided up into four main groups. The first in the supply chain were those who cut and shaped the limestone blocks in the nearby quarries. The second group used wooden rollers or ox-drawn sledges to haul the stones to the site, where the third team are presumed to have built massive ramps up the sides of the pyramid, enabling them to drag the stones up to the fourth team, who levered or otherwise manhandled them into position for eternity. Once the job was completed, the external ramps were removed to reveal the finished structure, standing ready for its final cladding in the white tiling slabs so long disappeared. All very neat and tidy to be sure, but this still fails to address the problem of how the millions of limestone blocks were cut in the first place or how they were 'trimmed' to abut so tightly, each taking into consideration the irregularities of its neighbours (if indeed the pyramids were built of natural stone blocks – not everyone accepts that they were).

PYRAMIDOLOGY

The mysticism ascribed the pyramids was born of the nineteenth-century pseudoscience of pyramidology, with Charles Piazzi Smyth, the Astronomer Royal for Scotland, spending the 1870s measuring every aspect and angle of the Great Pyramid to prove that it was an astronomical calculator.

Having documented all his measurements, Smyth worked backwards to his self-invented baseline of a presumed Sacred Inch, equivalent to 1.00106 British inches, and then worked forwards again to 'establish' that the perimeter of the Great Pyramid, as measured by himself, was exactly 36,524.2 Sacred Inches, or one-hundred times the number of solar days in the year. Dividing the height in Sacred Inches of any one side of the structure by 25 to arrive at his Sacred Cubit, the answer was a matching 365.242, and so forth.

In 1883, the Egyptologist Sir William Flinders Petrie established beyond any doubt that all of Smyth's measurements of the Great Pyramid were wildly inaccurate, and had been stretched or shortened to make them fit the procrustean bed of his Sacred Inch or Sacred Cubit theory.

The granite blocks from quarries at Aswan were most certainly the product of laborious cutting and shaping by labourers using hand-held wedges of extremely hard igneous rock to chip away the comparatively softer granite. Cut to form the lintels over access points and the galleries and chambers within, these were then shipped the 500-odd miles up the Nile and then through manmade canals to bring them as close as possible to the construction site, where they could only have been hauled into position by sheer weight of numbers. But this simply could not have been the case for the limestone blocks. The Great Pyramid was about twenty years in the making, which would have called for the production and installation of over 400 blocks per day. Estimates as to the size of the labour force working on the Great Pyramid have varied wildly over the years, with some placing it as high as 100,000 plus, but in 2002 this question at least was answered by the Giza Plateau Mapping Project.

Run by the universities of Chicago and Harvard, the project was led by archaeologist Mark Lehner, who uncovered a complex of individual dwellings and communal areas which, informally named Pyramid City, proved to be the township erected to accommodate that workforce. Estimated by Lehner to have accommodated no more than 20,000, if we eliminate wives and children we could then be left looking at a hands-on workforce of about 10,000. Although this core force was augmented by some of the agricultural workers rendered idle by the Nile's annual flood – from July to September – such a number would square with estimates as to how many men could physically fit onto such a construction site without, quite literally, falling over each other – the Great Pyramid at its base is only 230 metres square. So, could a workforce of such size produce, transport and instal 400 stone blocks a day? It's unlikely in the extreme. But there is a more recent theory that cuts through the Gordian knot of all the mysteries surrounding the construction of the pyramids.

Professor Joseph Davidovits, a French materials scientist of international recognition who is also acknowledged to be the founder of geopolymer chemistry, was first intrigued by the absence of any chippings and broken blocks at any of the limestone quarries either uphill from the Great Pyramid or at the wadi (a dry gully or valley) downhill from the site. Limestone is notorious for splitting when worked, so from the production of nearly three million blocks one would expect to find millions upon millions of chippings and shattered blocks. But he could find none. As a member of the International Association of Egyptologists, Davidovits started to look at the composition 'signature' of the limestone in the blocks of the Great Pyramid and soon established that this matched perfectly the 'signature' of the limestone at the wadi, leaving him to question the sanity of the ancient Egyptians' decision to source their limestone blocks from a quarry that lay downhill, which would make their transfer to the construction site all the more arduous. Once at the wadi, he immediately recognized this source to be one of soft limestone that bore no evidence of quarrying or carving, but of a gentler process of erosion and scouring to leave smooth and undulating surfaces. Next in his chain of discovery were hieroglyphics mentioning 'liquid stone' alongside drawings of men who seemed to be tamping down the contents of wooden boxes. So he again turned his attention to the blocks making up the Great Pyramid and realized that the fossil-shell deposits so typically found in limestone were not lying neatly as in natural sedimentary deposit, but all higgledy-piggledy as if they had been mixed up in fluid form. There was also irrefutable evidence of chemical reaction. Could the 'stones' actually be manmade blocks?

Davidovits theorized that limestone dust and rubble was brought up from the wadi to be dissolved in massive Nile-fed pools before being mixed with natron – a form of soda ash found in abundance in Egypt, where it was also used in the embalming of mummies. As the water evaporated the builders would have been left with a form of limestone cement to be carried up the structure in baskets for packing into moulds made of thin wooden slats, well-oiled on the inside so as not to stick to the block during the drying process. Once these initial blocks had quickly set under the Egyptian sun, they themselves would form the walls of the moulds for the casting of other blocks. As these new blocks set, each would undergo infinitesimal shrinkage to leave a 1 mm or 2 mm line between its formative neighbours to look for all the world like a finely crafted joint, which, to be fair, was exactly what it was. Moving on to the experimental stage, Davidovits made a few limestone blocks in this manner and not only did they present identical joint-lines to those on the Great Pyramid, but his blocks were indistinguishable to the naked eye from natural limestone.

In 2009, the Geopolymer Institute published Davidovits's revised *Why the Pharaohs Built the Pyramids with Fake Stone*, a book giving all the scientific data to back up his theory. In the same year, Michel Barsoum, Distinguished Professor of Materials Science at Drexel University and previously of the American University in Cairo, Egypt, decided to scan a few stones at the Giza pyramids with an electron microscope in an effort to prove his colleague wrong. Barsoum was more than a little surprised when his scan revealed air bubbles and natural fibres within the structure of his study blocks, two things that are never found within natural limestone. And so to who actually built the pyramids.

During his 1979 goodwill visit to Cairo, Israeli Prime Minister Menachem Begin upset his hosts by casually observing at the Pyramids, 'Of course, we built them.' Only in the Judaeo-Christian culture does the myth of Jewish slave labour's involvement stand prominent, which is surprising as the structures are not mentioned in the Bible or the Torah. Compounded into a widely accepted truth by countless movies and other media ventures, the myth was started by the Romano-Jewish historian Josephus, who, flourishing in the first century AD, used the fourth-century BC writings of Herodotus as his springboard.

With both men writing to their own agendum, Herodotus, who visited Egypt between 449 BC and 430 BC, deliberately set out to further denigrate the already tarnished reputation of Cheops, better known in his time as Khufu and the man who commissioned the Great Pyramid. Listing Khufu's many and mostly imaginary cruelties, Herodotus went on to say he was hated by his own people for pressing them into slavery to build the Great Pyramid as a monument to his own vanity.

Josephus's axe was altogether subtler and more complex in its grinding. Born Yosef ben Matityahu, he had been the commander of the Jewish forces in Galilee during the First Jewish–Roman War (AD 66–73) but was captured by the Emperor Vespasian, who kept him handy as a translator and advisor. Eventually assuming Roman citizenship, he wrote several works about the history of his own people, determined to present them to his adoptive nation as a noble and resourceful people with a devout and justified faith in one god. With the Romans by then having brought Egypt into their empire and so many of them travelling to see the oldest of the Seven Wonders of the Ancient World, it was easy to turn the 'slaves' mentioned by Herodotus into Jewish slaves to present them to the Roman reader as engineers of unbounded ability. But even Herodotus was wrong in that no slaves ever worked on the pyramids, as established by Lehner when examining the workers' complex he had discovered during the Giza Plateau Mapping Project. The rubbish dumps near the canteen-like dining areas showed they had a rich and varied diet and the burial chambers of the more elevated of their number indicated a reverential and respectful send-off that would never have been wasted on a slave. The arrival of the first Jews on Egyptian soil is noted in the Elephantine Papyri, a collection of 175 scrolls unearthed across the last part of the nineteenth century at the ruins of the ancient fortresses at Elephantine, an island in the Nile near Aswan, and at the fortress of Syene in Aswan itself. These note the local reaction to the arrival on the island of a significant number of Hebrew mercenaries in 650 BC when they took occupation of the fort before setting their Egyptian slaves to work on the building of a synagogue.

So, evidence does suggest that the pyramids were built by a dedicated and free Egyptian labour force who, if Professor Davidovits is right, cast their own 'Lego' bricks from limestone cement in ever-decreasing numbers as the structure rose higher and higher.

THE SPANISH INQUISITION: THE BLACK LEGEND

FOUNDED IN 1478 by Ferdinand II of Aragon and his wife, Isabella I of Castile, the very mention of the Inquisition, an office of the Spanish Catholic Church has, since the late sixteenth century, conjured up images of cruelty and persecution. We have all seen the cinematic portrayals of hooded clerics torturing a terrified and naked woman or seen one of the countless Bruegel-like representations of an Inquisition interrogation chamber. The reality was very different, so who created these lies and why?

With the word 'Spanish' so inexorably linked to 'Inquisition', most of us have been left with the impression that this was the only such office. But in fact Spain was a late starter, with the first Inquisition instituted by twelfth-century France to deal with the rise of the heretical Cathars. In its day, every Catholic country – from Portugal to Peru – raised an Inquisition, so why was the Spanish one singled out for so much vilification despite its having been perhaps the most lenient of all? The answer lies in the abhorrence with which the rest of Europe regarded the rise of sixteenth-century Spain to a position of military and maritime supremacy, and the subversive activities of those same Protestant propagandists responsible for the myth of Pope Joan (see page 35). While the Spanish Inquisitors were not the most liberal-minded bunch of chaps one would have been likely to encounter in Spain across the fifteenth and sixteenth centuries, they proved the perfect whipping boys for the rest of Western Europe, anxious to blacken the name of Spain and distract attention from the fact that Protestant countries were beginning to torture and burn witches and heretics on a scale that would have made any Inquisitor's eyes water.

At first, the Protestants raised armies to attack Catholic forces in the conventional manner but, after their complete rout at the Battle of Mühlberg in 1547 at the hands of Charles, Ferdinand and Isabella's grandson, they realized that this was not their best option. So the Protestants attacked Spain with a weapon against which it had little or no defence – the printing press. They churned out pamphlets and gothic etchings in their thousands to besmirch the name of Spain and that of its Inquisition, presenting the reader with tales and images of such outlandish cruelty it is a wonder that any believed a word of it. Many of the enduring myths surrounding early torture can be traced back to such pamphlets – the non-existent iron maiden, for example – whereas the torture instruments of such time were barbarically basic (if highly effective). Eventually, the Protestant propagandists played their ace in the form of a book entitled *A Discovery and Playne Declaration of Sundry Subtill Practices of The Holy Inquisition of Spayne* (1567), ostensibly by one

Reginaldus Montanus, who claimed to have endured the brutality of the Spanish Inquisition and witnessed the deviant horrors visited on others – especially women. Despite the book being pure bunkum and the author proving untraceable, the work was immediately translated for pan-European distribution to disseminate what the Spanish still call the Black Legend. The fact that one can still buy reproductions of that book from most online book vendors speaks volumes of its impact.

In reality, the Spanish Inquisition was perhaps the most even-handed and least brutal of all such institutions as a meticulous trawl through its extensive records stored in Salamanca has suggested. Examined by many, but most notably by Professors Henry Kamen and Jaime Contreras of the Barcelona Higher Council for Scientific Research and the Spanish University of Alcalá respectively, the Salamanca records prove that the Spanish Inquisition was never the sadistic playground of sexually deviant clerics in pointy, KKK-style hats. The vast majority of Spanish Inquisitors were secular lawyers who not only insisted on hard proof of transgression but who also had to work within some very clearly defined parameters. Nor was the Inquisition an instrument of persecution aimed at Jews, Muslims and members of other faiths; the Spanish Inquisition had jurisdiction over Catholics and Catholics alone (even if some of those Catholics were Jews who had effectively been forced to convert).

Apart from dealing with heresy or crimes of faith, the Inquisition was also active in the prosecution of adultery, bigamy, sodomy and other moral issues, all the way down to breach of promise, public drunkenness and swearing in church. And its aforementioned leniency made it a highly desirable alternative to those in the grip of the civil system, many of whom opted to sit in court shouting blasphemies until the judge had no choice but to hand them over to the Inquisition, whose prisons were the best in Europe. The much maligned Inquisitor-in-chief, Tomás de Torquemada, insisted on a regime of cleanliness, decent food, a change of clothes for all inmates and a considerable degree of protection for female prisoners to save them from the unwelcome attentions of their jailers and other inmates. It is a matter of record that on at least two occasions, when the Inquisition jails of Barcelona and Salamanca were overflowing, both refused to hand over some of their charges to the local civil jails as they thought them inhumane; instead, they simply released some of the low-level prisoners on receiving promise of their return in a few months. There was a much better chance of survival when investigated by the Spanish Inquisition rather than the civil courts, which were frequently nothing more than a thin veneer of legality for some baying mob set on a lynching.

That said, to attract the attention of the Spanish Inquisition in its early days was no laughing matter; it most certainly had some very sharp teeth it was not afraid to use. Its inception had been inspired by the desire of Ferdinand and Isabella to see a Spain of unified faith, so the considerable population of Spanish Jewry was given a period of grace to decide whether to leave the country or remain as *conversos*, Jews converted to the Catholic faith. Some Spaniards believed – and not without justification – that many *conversos* were simply paying lip-service to Catholicism while continuing to practise their real faith in secret. And, of course, there

---

TOMÁS DE TORQUEMADA

With the first element of his surname rather ironically bearing strong etymological links to other words such as 'twist' and 'torture', Tomás de Torquemada was perhaps an obvious target for the Protestant black propaganda machine.

A Dominican friar of Jewish descent, at the age of sixty-three Torquemada was appointed Grand Inquisitor in 1483 and, while the very mention of his name conjures up images of thousands burning to death at the stake, he only held office for fifteen years, with the last five of those years spent at home in bed due to ill health. The Spanish Inquisition, on the other hand, was in business for over 350 years.

Although he was a dogged persecutor of heretics, from all accounts Torquemada was dour but fair. He ensured the prisons of the Inquisition were sanitary and his trials even-handed, with the burden of proof on the prosecution.

---

was also the usual anti-Semitic envy of their wealth, which would fall forfeit if they were found guilty of such crimes. With the Spanish Inquisition structured to be self-funding through the fines and confiscations harvested by its own judgements, some groundless prosecutions must have been inflicted but, on balance, it must also be said that across those first fifteen years executions only ran to about 130 per annum which, abhorrent by modern standards, has to be seen in the context of the times. Many of those tried were indeed guilty of heresy, then considered a grave crime. By contrast and across the same period, the rest of Western Europe slaughtered perhaps 60,000 witches and heretics. Despite the English Henry VIII now promoted as a jolly fine fellow, the man was a paranoid thug; apart from those who were executed for matters of faith or heresy, during his thirty-seven-year reign he imposed tens of thousands of further secular executions.

On 18 April 1482 Pope Sixtus IV sent a letter to the Council of Bishops of Spain to bid them to be wary of avarice tainting their Inquisition through the malicious prosecution of converted Jews or other wealthy targets perceived as vulnerable. Although Ferdinand wrote back to inform the Pope in no uncertain terms that such accusations were groundless and that he should mind his own holy business, he nevertheless appointed Tomás de Torquemada in 1483 to oversee the actions of the Spanish Inquisition and make sure it could never stand accused of such base motives.

Although major cities had static offices of the Inquisition there were also travelling offices which toured towns and villages too small to warrant a permanent presence and, another indication as to the leniency of the Spanish Inquisition, these peripatetic offices almost proved their own undoing. Knowing that the average Spanish countryman was largely unaware of its existence or the scope and reach of its judgements, the travelling Inquisition felt it only fair to alert rural towns and villages of its impending arrival and to further announce an edict of grace to give everyone thirty days to draw up a list of any minor sin or transgression weighing on their mind so they could, on the Inquisition's arrival, present themselves for confession and absolution. But this backfired big-time. Terrified out of their wits, the collective Spanish peasantry rushed to meet the Inquisition at every stop with endless lists of actual transgressions, any transgressions of which others might *think* them guilty, or any false accusations their enemies might think to throw in their direction. Thus clogged with such a caseload, the travelling Inquisitions frequently opted to issue a blanket absolution to every living soul in the area before beating a hasty retreat from the tsunami of would-be penitents flooding towards them. This was the beginning of the Inquisition becoming a victim of its own leniency.

Although the Spanish Inquisition was designed to be self-funding through its fines and confiscations, the various offices, each with one legal advisor, one constable, a prosecuting lawyer and at least a dozen or so support staff, were frequently left begging subsidies from the Crown just to meet the wages bill. Throughout its 350 years of operation the Spanish Inquisition tried something just short of 250,000 cases, resulting in about 4,000 executions – on average about a dozen a year. The vast majority of Inquisition cases resulted in acquittals. The Spanish Inquisition did indeed use torture, but so did everyone else back then and records show that it only resorted to such tactics in fewer than 2 per cent of all cases. When torture was employed it was restricted to a maximum of fifteen minutes and could only be repeated once; no one ever endured a third round and only half of the aforementioned 2 per cent received their second dose.

These were the days when English dungeons were always stocked with racks and thumbscrews and a starving waif from the streets of London could be hanged for stealing a loaf of bread. Across the sixteenth and seventeenth centuries, England hanged between 400 and 2,000 'witches' – despite what one sees in films, such victims were never burned at the stake in England – while Protestant Germany had a much higher number. The Spanish Inquisition, by contrast, had declared early that belief in witches and witchcraft was a silly delusion so none could be tried for it or punished in any way; they further warned that anyone bringing imaginary accusations of witchery against another would end up on charges themselves. So, although shocking by today's standards, set against the activities of the rest of

Western Europe at that time, it is clear that the real facts surrounding the activities of the Spanish Inquisition do not match the myth.

———◇———

RAISING THE ROOF:
THE MANY INCARNATIONS
OF STONEHENGE

SECOND ONLY TO the pyramids of Egypt, Stonehenge has been the subject of more conjecture than any other structure on the planet. Across the past few centuries several sub-cultures – most notably the Neo-Druids, the Wicca Movement and assorted pagans – have tried to appropriate the stone circle, claiming it to have been a temple or gathering point for their faith. There is no evidence, however, to suggest Stonehenge ever fulfilled such a function. As to why the circle provokes so much fascination, that is perhaps best summed up by the late British archaeologist Jacquetta Hawkes, wife of J. B. Priestley and the first woman ever to study her subject at Cambridge University. Seeing the site as a mirror onto which successive cultures have projected their fears or dreams, Hawkes once famously quipped that every age gets the Stonehenge it deserves. In the Middle Ages it was believed to have been built by giants labouring under the direction of Merlin; in the eighteenth and nineteenth centuries, which saw the rise of interest in the Druidic culture, it was a place of Druid worship and sacrifice; and, in the 1960s at the threshold of the computer age, it was perceived as a giant calculator.

That said, with evidence of other construction work in the immediate area dating back some 9,000 years, Stonehenge itself was not a single project but a collection of enterprises completed in four distinct phases spanning 1,500 years. There is considerable debate over the dating of these stages of construction, with some electing to divide phase 3 into multiple stages. But, to keep things simple, we are here opting for four stages with approximate dating.

Phase 1 commenced around 3000 BC with the laying out of the circular ditch and bank and the circle of fifty-six 1-metre-square pits dug into the chalk, possibly for tall wooden poles. These are today generally known as the Aubrey Holes after John Aubrey, the seventeenth-century antiquarian who first wrote of pits and depressions at Stonehenge. However, there is now significant doubt as to whether the pits so briefly mentioned by Aubrey were in fact the same ones as comprise this purpose-made circle of pits – 284 feet in diameter – which surround the later-installed stones. Phase 2 began *c.* 2500 BC with the importation of some eighty-odd so-called bluestones from the Preseli Mountains in south-west Wales, about 250 miles away. Weighing approximately 4 tons each, this importation of stones was itself no mean feat of logistics. With the intention of forming two concentric circles of standing monoliths, work seems to have ground to a halt leaving one of the circles incomplete. It was during this phase that a wider breach was cut in the circular bank to allow access to the inner site. Phase 3 saw the

arrival of the massive standing stones and lintels brought in from quarries at Avebury in Wiltshire, about 25 miles to the north. It has been estimated that it would have taken about 500 men with log-rollers and skids to move each stone to the site, where they were arranged in a lintel-topped circle with five trilithons setting out an inner circle. Then during phase 4, *c.* 2300 BC, the incomplete circle of bluestones was rearranged into a horseshoe within the completed circle of its fellows before the site underwent further alterations. Stonehenge was then abandoned to its long and slow journey into decay and dilapidation.

It is important to bear the above in mind when assessing assertions as to the purpose of Stonehenge – it was a computer; it was a solar tracker; it was an astronomical observatory – because such postulations are put forward as if the monument's construction was a single project overseen by a single culture following the dictates of a specific plan or agendum. Instead, this was a multi-stage project completed over hundreds of years, with those involved in each successive stage neither knowing nor careful of the purpose or intention of their predecessors. The initial and circular groundworks of the ditch and mound were carried out by the Windmill Hill People, an ancient culture of Salisbury Plain of whom little else is known; next came the Beaker People with the Wessex People, adding the finishing touches *c*. 1500 BC. Furthermore, what we see today at Stonehenge is not the pattern it presented in its original form as that is now lost for ever. Similar to the stone circle at nearby Avebury, where the larger stones for Stonehenge were sourced, many argue that what we see today at both sites is in fact a twentieth-century creation.

Neither Stonehenge nor Avebury came under the protection of the National Trust or English Heritage until the early twentieth century; before this, and most certainly in the case of Avebury, the stones were regarded either as irksome impediments to the ploughing of the land or as 'freebie' stones to be smashed into smaller pieces for other works. In 1934, the jam magnate Alexander Keiller used his considerable wealth to acquire the entire 950-acre site at Avebury, complete with the village, and set about what can best be described as a programme of destructive reconstruction to form what he thought the site must have looked like 5,000 years ago. Unfettered by the kind of budgetary restraints so often the bane of more formal archaeological projects, the flamboyant Keiller set about the reconstruction of his 1-mile circumference 'Neolithic' stone circle, with its two inner rings, in a manner that would whiten the hair of any modern archaeologist.

His labours were captured on footage shot across 1937–9 by Avebury resident Percy Lawes and transferred to video in the 1970s for posterity. The films show Keiller and his team demolishing dozens of homes and farm buildings to make way for the pattern he envisioned, with the wrong stones being set in concrete within existing pits that had to be dramatically reshaped to accept their new occupants while 'new' stones were installed into purpose-dug pits to complete the pattern that Keiller had in mind. It now transpires that Keiller's vision was indeed impaired. A joint project conducted in 2017 by the universities of Leicester and Southampton, using the latest in ground-penetrating radar, has revealed that, originally, there was at the centre of the site a 30-metre square of stones laid out about the central monolith. Such deviation from the circular, according to Dr Mark Gillings, Academic Director of Archaeology at Leicester University, is unique in megalithic monuments.

As for Stonehenge, although the site is considerably smaller than that of Avebury, much the same 're-imaginings' have likewise been imposed, albeit to a lesser degree. Any reader caring to conduct a quick internet search for John Constable's 1835 depiction of the site will see the majority of the stones lying in a state of collapse and those still standing tilted to a precarious angle. It was clear that this was no artistic interpretation of the ravages of time, as borne out by early photographs of the site showing the stones in an even more advanced state of collapse. With the site attracting a broader domestic and international interest

---

LOT 15

Stonehenge belonged to the Priory of Amesbury until 1536 when Henry VIII confiscated all monastic properties and granted ownership of the Amesbury estates to the Earl of Hereford, after whom the lands, along with the derelict monument, passed through the hands of several titled families, including that of the Marquis of Queensberry.

In 1824 the monument and the surrounding 30 acres of land was bought by the Antrobus family of Cheshire who built several cottages and even a café (later demolished) close to the stones. When the last of the Antrobus line was killed in the First World War, the whole parcel of land was put up for auction in September 1915.

Presented for sale as 'Lot 15', it was bought for £6,000 by Sir Cecil Chubb, who had been sent to the sale room by his wife, her heart set on a dining table and chair set that had been advertised. Apparently Lady Chubb was less than impressed by his acquisition, and Sir Cecil donated the land to the nation in 1918.

---

at the turn of the twentieth century, work began in 1901 to 'tidy up' the monument, a move unpopular in many quarters. The letters column of *The Times* abounded with protests at such 'desecration' but the restoration continued with additional phases imposed in 1919 and 1920, and again in 1958–9. The finishing touches were finally made in 1964, by which time 'new' lintel stones had been added and, according to Christopher Chippindale, Senior Curator at the Cambridge University Museum of Archaeology and Anthropology, virtually all the other stones moved or repositioned in some way before being set in concrete.

Thus we have a twentieth-century imagining of what the monument might have looked like thousands of years ago. At the turn of the present century, David Batchelor, Senior Archaeologist at English Heritage, acknowledged that in the 1960s a decision had been taken not to detail the renovations and restorative work in the guide books but that this error of omission would now be addressed. This aggressive restoration and repositioning of stones also calls into question the various claims of certain stones' celestial and solar alignments as the original layout may have been different. So, that just leaves a final question – did Stonehenge ever have a roof?

Just as changes in fashion keep the tills ringing in clothes shops, new theories are the lifeblood of academic archaeology. The most recent speculation surrounding Stonehenge proposes that it was not always just a circle of stones but spent time as an actual building. To paraphrase Sarah Ewbank, a prominent landscape architect with a long-term interest in the site, why go to all that effort to erect a simple circle of stones so you can put on your best goatskins to dance round it at the summer and winter solstices when you can put a roof on it and use the building all the year round? And she is not alone in such speculation. In the late 1990s, Dr Timothy Darvill, Professor of Archaeology at Bournemouth University and an acknowledged authority on Stonehenge, gave tentative support to the notion, but he has since distanced himself from the roof theory. Yet Dr Julian Spalding, in his time the director of some of the UK's leading museums, favours the suggestion that the outer circle of stones at one time acted as supports for some sort of super-structure, while Dr Aubrey Burl, previously Principal Lecturer in Archaeology at Hull College and himself an acknowledged expert on Neolithic monuments, has cautiously opined that the roof theory is not without its merits and possibilities.

Supporters of the roof theory point out that the lintels of the outer circle were locked onto the top of the upright stones with double mortise-and-tenon joints, as if they were intended to absorb the kind of lateral stress that would have been exerted by vaulted timber work supporting a thatched roof. Had this not been the case then the weight of the stones themselves would have been sufficient to keep them in position, so such jointing only makes sense if super-structural additions were anticipated. It has also been suggested that the timber posts set into the aforementioned Aubrey Holes might have supported some kind of external veranda encircling the finished structure.

But, for the time being at least, the roof theory is destined to languish in the realm of speculation as any such thatching and timber supports would long since have rotted away.

5

Conflict and Catastrophe

THE BLACK HOLE OF CALCUTTA: A LIE BUILT ON GREED

THE BARE BONES of this alleged atrocity are well known in both the UK and India but the incident itself was at best the subject of gross exaggeration and at worst one of cynical invention by the East India Company (EIC), anxious for public and governmental backing to expand its already colossal corporate influence across the subcontinent.

Founded by a royal charter issued by Elizabeth I on 31 December 1600, by the eighteenth century the EIC had grown into a giant to dwarf any conglomerate of the twenty-first century. Most worryingly for many, not only had it grown beyond the control of any government but the company had its own army and navy dwarfing those of the British regular forces. At its peak in the 1850s, the EIC had over 271,000 troops under its command and many more ships under sail than the British Navy. By 1756 it was throwing its weight around in Calcutta, now Kolkata, flouting its agreements with the local ruler or Nawab of Bengal, Siraj ud-Daulah, and interfering in the internal affairs of his realm. When the company also embarked on major expansions of its fortified power base in the city, Fort William, Siraj ud-Daulah's well-founded suspicions as to why this was being done prompted him to attack the installation on 20 June that year.

Most of the company troops and local recruits deserted and fled, so there were comparatively few left in the fort when the Nawab's forces stormed the place; the exact number of Europeans who were locked up in the fort's jail, known to locals as the Black Hole, remains unknown. When the Nawab entered the fort he immediately informed the senior EIC officer on site, John Zephaniah Holwell, that no harm would befall any of them and that, if they gave their word to behave, they could remain at large and unmolested within the confines of the fort. However, no sooner had the Nawab left the fort than the Europeans turned so petulant and demanding that the Nawab's men slung the ringleaders – Holwell included, if he is to be believed – into the company's own loathsome jail to teach them a lesson. The lowest estimate holds this contingent to

have numbered nine, with three of them dead by morning – not from anything diabolical visited upon them by their captors but from wounds received during their short-lived and lacklustre defence of the fort the previous day. However, the incensed Holwell, determined to see the EIC reassert its stranglehold on the area and extend its tentacles into the neighbouring provinces, returned to London to publish *A Genuine Narrative of the Deplorable Deaths of the English Gentlemen and Others Who Were Suffocated in The Black Hole.*

According to this account – which Holwell cobbled together with other executives of the EIC who were not even in India at the time – 146 people went into the Hole and, in the morning, only 23 staggered out. Not only was there nothing like that number of Europeans left in the fort when it fell but the Hole itself measured a scant 18 feet by 14 feet and was thus incapable of holding such numbers. And there were other problems with Holwell's lurid account of his night of horror. Droning on in ridiculous embellishment, he detailed the wretched faces of his companions twisted in pain and desperation for the water that the sniggering jailers kept pouring into the sand before their very eyes and so forth. The jail was not called the Black Hole for nothing; there were only two small ventilation slits, so how could he have seen such details in the total darkness that gave the jail its name? The great British public was in no mood for any such logical questioning of Holwell's penny dreadful; the Nawab needed a damned good thrashing. It was time to unleash the beast that was Robert Clive, aka Clive of India.

THE FATE OF ROBERT CLIVE

For all his ill-gotten wealth, Robert Clive was destined to die in London in mysterious circumstances, discovered in his Berkeley Square mansion on 22 November 1774. Strangely, there was no inquest and rumours circulated of his having cut his own throat or died from a self-administered overdose of opium. Who knows, perhaps some of his old Market Drayton victims finally caught up with him; either way he was buried in an unmarked grave in the parish church at Moreton Say, close to his birthplace. A good indicator as to the scale of the loot he plundered was given by his descendants putting up for sale six items of Moghul art at Christie's in 2004 which sold for £4.7 million; not bad for a small-town bully boy!

This was exactly the reaction for which the EIC had been hoping; the public howling for blood to such a degree that none in the government dared impose any restriction on the degree of EIC retaliation and, in Robert Clive, they had just the man for the job. Born into the family estates at Market Drayton in Shropshire, Clive had a reputation as a thug with a passion for street-fighting. He also ran a protection racket in the town and surrounding areas; owners of shops and businesses who did not relish waking up to a raging fire had no choice but to pay up. By the time he was eighteen, Market Drayton in general and his own family in particular had endured enough and so they packed him off to India with a post in the EIC. He later joined the company's army. Rising meteorically through the ranks, Clive was mistaken by others to have been a bold and valiant commander, but he remained a thug, only now he had an army with which to play instead of a street gang. Already addicted to opium, he displayed an almost criminal disregard for his own and others' safety.

Having recaptured Fort William and soundly trashed the forces of the Nawab, Clive moved on to bring other provinces under the EIC umbrella by employing much the same tactics he had used as a teenager in Market Drayton. Those who wanted to play ball with the EIC, as puppet rulers, had to pay him a huge bounty in return for the use of his army to crush those hostile to the prospect. These bribes, augmented by what he looted along the way, allowed Clive to return to the UK a very rich man indeed. With much of India back in the malevolent and avaricious grip of the EIC, few dared question the veracity of the Holwell account that had instigated the Clive-led backlash. Not until 1915 did the first cogent rebuttal emerge in the form of *The Black Hole – The Question of Holwell's Veracity*, published by J. H. Little, Secretary of the Calcutta Historical Society. This was followed a few decades later by detailed papers from the likes of Ramesh Chandra Majumdar, Vice-Chancellor of Dacca University, and Basudeb Chattopadhyay, Professor of Modern Indian History and Director of the West Bengal State Archives. When the British finally began their disastrous exit of India in 1947, their Black Hole Monument to Indian brutality and ingratitude was one of the first offensive reminders of their presence to be torn down by the mob.

INVASIONS OF THE SPANISH CONQUISTADORS: THE INCAS AND THE IRISH

THE GREATEST PUZZLE confronting the first-time visitor to South America is the pronounced Irish influence on the culture. It is notable in Chile, for instance, that there are several statues raised up to the incongruously named Bernardo O'Higgins (1778–1842) who, from a family hailing from County Sligo, is still venerated as the Father of Chilean Independence and the first Supreme Director of the country after emancipating it from Spanish control. Likewise, tourists in Argentina may be equally surprised by the plethora of Irish pubs and restaurants there, and it is much the same in Brazil where the statue of Christ the Redeemer above Rio is bathed in shamrock-green light every St Patrick's Day, accompanied by huge celebrations in the city. The foundations for these ongoing ties binding South America and Ireland date back to the early 1500s when Spain and the counties to the south of Ireland formed strong trading associations, resulting in a little-known but significant Irish diaspora that followed in the footsteps of the Spanish Conquistadors who invaded Mexico and South America in that same century.

The bare bones of the history of the Spanish invasions of Mexico by Hernan Cortez in 1519 and South America by Francisco Pizarro across the 1520s are as well known as they are misperceived. In each case the invading force is believed to have been pitifully small yet triumphant through their innate superiority to the Inca and the Mexican Aztec, who were so benighted that they thought the Spanish with their comparatively pale skin to be the incarnations of their own pagan gods. Needless to say, the truth is very different. Indeed, it is stretching the point even to call those two invading forces Spanish; they certainly did not consider themselves such. That which we call Spain was at the time an uneasy alliance of independent realms only given a veneer of unity by the 1469 marriage of Isabella of Castile and Ferdinand of Aragon. But this still left Catalonia, the Basque Lands, Murcia, Andalusia, Valencia and several other historic regions of 'Spain' being gradually forced into a union for which they had little desire. This uneasy unification is still apparent in modern-day Spain, highlighted by the ongoing terror campaign of the Basque separatists known as ETA and the separatists' vote of 2017 carrying the day in Catalonia. Then, as indeed now, most in Spain identified themselves first by their region of origin.

Cortez was from Extremadura and Pizarro from Castile. In the case of Pizarro, he did not, as many imagined, simply land in Peru in 1526 and take it over. A piratical adventurer, he had already made several trips to South America and in Panama picked up on tales of gold aplenty in Peru. But his 1524 invasion of that country was successfully denied by the native population. He tried again in 1526 but had no sooner landed than he was recalled by a ship sent after him by Pedro de los Rios, the Governor of Panama. Reluctant to retreat yet again, this is when Pizarro allegedly drew a line in the sand on the beach with the tip of his sword inviting 'all good Castilians' present to indicate their resolve to remain in Peru with him by stepping over it. The few who elected to remain with him in Peru are celebrated in Spanish history as the Famous Thirteen, which did much to promote the myth that Pizarro subjugated the whole of Peru with the help of only twelve men. In fact, even this attempt at establishing a Peruvian foothold was unsuccessful, forcing Pizarro and his Famous Thirteen to return to Panama with their collective tails between their legs. Undaunted, Pizarro left his men there while he returned to Madrid to convince Charles V, the Holy Roman Emperor, who doubled as Charles I of Spain, that there was much gold just waiting to be taken. He was granted a charter, three fully provisioned ships, artillery and 180 men-at-arms.

With such strength Pizarro returned to Peru where, now forearmed with the knowledge that none of the other tribes cared for the high-handed Inca, he soon managed to raise a native army of over 35,000. And it was much the same for Cortez, who likewise found little trouble in raising a local army of over 200,000 to assist in his campaigns against the all-powerful Aztecs. So much for the myth.

As for the equally widely held notion that the Aztec leader, Montezuma, thought Cortez to be the incarnation of Quetzalcoatl, the feathered serpent god, and that the

Incas thought Pizarro to be the living image of their god, Viracocha, and that both tribes showered their invaders with gold, this was invented by Spanish historians to cover up the wholesale slaughter inflicted by both men in their brutal quest for ever more wealth. There is not a shred of evidence to support this claim and much to refute it. The story only rears its head decades after the events and it is hard to believe that the Inca and the Aztec could mistake the horrendous behaviour and decidedly mortal 'appetites' of their invaders for that of divine proclivity.

Pizarro and those who followed in his murderous footsteps also failed in finding the one thing they all sought – the fabled city they called El Dorado. This was not because El Dorado did not exist, but because the Spanish had taken a masterly grasp on the wrong end of the stick when it came to the legend. El Dorado was not a city, but in fact a man. Prior to the inauguration of a new Inca leader, the king-to-be had to spend days in contemplative isolation before being stripped naked and coated in honey or oil so that copious amounts of gold dust would stick to every part of his body to present him to his people as the Golden King or the Golden One. But the invading Spanish convinced themselves that El Dorado, as they called it, was a city groaning with gold, and they started to interrogate captives as to its location. But the problem with torture is that the victim will quickly tell you whatever it is you want to hear in order to gain respite from the pain, and countless Inca kept telling their inquisitors that the city of El Dorado did indeed exist – but far, far away.

GUEVARA IN LIMERICK

Patrick Lynch of Galway moved to Buenos Aires in 1749 with his direct descendant Ernesto Lynch, born in 1928, later being better known to the world as the Marxist revolutionary Che Guevara. Inordinately proud of his Irish heritage, Guevara broke his Prague–New York flight at Shannon Airport on 13 March 1965 so he could join in the pre-St Patrick's Day celebrations in nearby Limerick. Drinkers in Hanratty's Hotel stood slack-jawed in amazement as he wandered up to the bar in his trademark camouflage fatigues and asked for a pint of Guinness.

From here he went on a pub crawl with Arthur Quinlan of the Dublin *Sunday Tribune* and the pair of them ended up at The White Horse on O'Connell Street with Guevara so drunk he could hardly stand. Quinlan recalled he had deliberately stayed sober in the hope of getting some information, but his drunken companion let nothing slip – apart from the fact that he could speak English, something he always denied in interviews.

So, the Spanish went to South America in search of gold and their long-term trading partners from Ireland tagged along for the ride, resulting in Argentina, for example, now playing host to the fifth-largest Irish population in the world. It is well known that, in times of trouble and famine, many Irish headed for New York and Chicago – but these were mostly from the north of Ireland. Those from the south made for Spain, Mexico or South America.

One such early escapee was William Lamport from County Wexford who, in 1630, sailed to Spain and then on to Mexico where, in 1641, he became involved in the independence movement, with his flamboyant antics the likely inspiration for the fictional character Zorro. There is even a statue of Lamport in the Monument to Independence in Mexico City. During the 1846–8 war between the United States and Mexico, hundreds of Irish troops in the US Army deserted and crossed over into Mexico to establish the St Patrick's Battalion, still remembered as freedom fighters in both Mexico and Ireland to this day.

This Hispanic–Irish fusion can also be seen in reverse. The first Prime Minister of the Republic of Ireland, established in 1918, was Eamon de Valera, born in the Americas of an Irish mother and a Basque father. In 1806, when Britain tried to take control of a vast tract of Argentinian territory in what was known as the Invasion of the River Plate, all the Irish soldiers in the invasion force deserted and went over to the Argentinian army. During the Easter Rising of 1916, it was a man from Argentina who raised the flag of Independent Ireland above the General Post Office in Dublin (after the rising was crushed, Eamon Bulfin was deported, later to be appointed Irish Consul in Buenos Aires by the aforementioned Eamon de Valera). And such ties still bind, as shown by the Irish stance during the Falklands conflict between the UK and Argentina. Drawing accusations of treason and treachery from the popular press, the Haughey government condemned the British sinking of the *General Belgrano* and pressed the UN Security Council for an immediate ceasefire.

And it seems these links between Spain and Ireland run deeper than merely reciprocal trade deals in the sixteenth century. His work duplicated and confirmed by further studies conducted by universities in Norway and Spain, Dr Daniel G. Bradley of the Genetics Department at Trinity College Dublin recently revealed that, genetically, the closest living relatives of the Irish are none other than the Basques of Northern Spain, such findings resonating with an old legend of the Irish claiming them all to be descended from the sons of a man called Milesius, who is said to have come to Ireland from Spain before the time of Christ. On a darker note, it has long been known that *Phytophthora infestans* was the fungus responsible for the Great Potato Famine of 1845 that drove the Irish diaspora, but historically no one knew how it came to Ireland. Researchers have now discovered that it came from South America and most likely arrived on Spanish boats trading into Irish ports.

—◆◇◆—

THE LIGHT BRIGADE:
A CHARGED-UP FAMILY FEUD

IT IS SAID, and perhaps rightly so, that only the British can turn a military fiasco into an event of national pride, and none more so than with the abortive Charge of the Light Brigade of 25 October 1854 during the Crimean War, which saw the combined forces of Turkey, France and Britain pitted against the might of the Russian Empire. But why did a single brigade of British cavalry embark upon a head-on attack against a full array of Russian artillery that was itself defended by several brigades of Cossack cavalry? The British chose to remember the event as an example of the stiff upper lip of unquestioning obedience of the nineteenth-century military – 'theirs not to reason why – theirs but to do and die', to quote the poetic celebration of the event by Alfred, Lord Tennyson. It was in reality one blunder too far, which called into question the entire command structure of the British Army. In the main, the fiasco was occasioned by a long-standing feud between two brothers-in-law and the abject horror with which the military elite viewed the rise of the professional soldier.

During the Battle of Balaklava, the Russians overran three Turkish emplacements on the Causeway Heights. Watching from his command post, Lord Raglan, the man in overall charge of the British forces on the peninsula, thought the Russians were making ready to haul away the captured artillery so he hurriedly dictated an order to his quarter-master general, General Richard Airey, who just happened to be standing nearby. This still-extant scrap of paper read, 'Lord Raglan wishes the cavalry to advance rapidly to the front, follow the enemy, and try to prevent the enemy carrying away the guns. Troop Horse Artillery may accompany. French cavalry is on your left. R Airey. Immediate'. The note was handed to Airey's aide, Captain Nolan, with the verbal overrider, 'Tell Lord Lucan that the cavalry are to attack immediately.' So, off galloped Nolan with the highly ambiguous order. In the 1968 cinematic portrayal of the event, with Sir John Gielgud taking the part of Raglan, his character watches Nolan leaving with the observation that he distrusted Nolan as 'he knows his job too well. It will be a sad day, Airey, when England has her armies officered by men who know too well what they are doing. It smacks of murder.' Although claimed by the producers to be a direct quote, such attribution to Raglan cannot be found. But even if these words were a dramatic flourish in the film script, they neatly encapsulate the attitude of the aristocratic military elite to the rise of men like Nolan, who actually knew what they were about on the battlefield.

Born in Canada, Nolan was a lowly colonial who had also seen service in India in postings not held in high regard by most high-ranking officers. Much to their annoyance, he also took a professional approach to the business of soldiery and war. He cared for the wellbeing of the horses and the men, and had written much on matters of strategy and the need to unclutter the prevailing military uniforms, the dangling attachments of which presented serious problems to those forced to wear them while riding, fighting or moving through shrub or forested terrain. He also openly condemned the purchase system whereby anyone with the money could buy both rank and the command of a regiment. While those in the corridors of power saw this as a way of ensuring that control of the army remained in the hands of the upper

classes, it also meant that thousands of regular soldiers died needlessly due to the ignorance of many high-ranking officers with no warfare experience and little common sense. Lord Cardigan, who had bought the colonelcy of the 11th Hussars for £40,000 before spending another fortune to make them the most 'fashionable' unit in the army, took personal exception to Nolan's opinions on such matters.

When Nolan delivered Raglan's order to Lucan, who was in overall sub-command of the cavalry units, the Causeway Heights were obscured from his view by the local geography, causing him to complain that he could see neither enemy nor guns. Nolan was in equally hostile mood and, careless of where he was pointing, gestured not in the direction of the Causeway Heights but straight down the North Valley to the massed Russian artillery over a mile away. 'There, my Lord, is your enemy and there are your guns.' And that was that. Lucan rode over to hand on the order to his detested brother-in-law, Lord Cardigan, at the head of the Light Brigade and it is fair to say that, had he and Lucan not been at such loggerheads, a dialogue would have ensued to question the sanity of such orders before demanding clarification. As it was, they just stood snarling at each other with Lucan barely able to disguise his glee at the prospect of his arch-enemy about to be flung into the jaws of hell ready to devour him at the head of the North Valley. Although he was meant to lead his Heavy Brigade in support of Cardigan, Lucan had no intention of enjoining such folly; he simply led his brigade to the mouth of the North Valley and watched the Light Brigade disappear into the cloud of their own dust.

As the Light Brigade moved off in the wrong direction, Nolan, noting the misinterpretation of the order, rode after them, calling for them to turn left, but he was almost immediately killed by shrapnel from a shell-burst to leave the Light Brigade to its fate. The Russians simply couldn't believe their eyes; a 670-strong division of light cavalry heading straight for them; surely they would wheel away at any moment to attack elsewhere; but they just kept coming. Despite withering fire from three sides, the brigade made it to the guns with Cardigan, in the lead, jumping over the Russian artillery to find himself staring at Prince Mikhail Radziwill, an officer in the Russian army with whom Cardigan had been on friendly terms in the social circuits of London before the war. The two men exchanged a smart salute before Cardigan jumped back over the guns to ride for home, passing on his way the last of the stragglers still making for the Russian line. A fine illustration of the thinking and attitude of Cardigan and others of his ilk is provided by his later explanation that, having led the men to their objective, he considered his duty done and saw no need to tarry and 'fight the enemy amongst private soldiers'. Having nothing better to do, he repaired to his yacht in Balaklava harbour to enjoy a champagne dinner.

Those members of the Light Brigade who managed to break through the line of Russian guns to be taken prisoner were held in awe by the Russians, who kept asking if they were all roaring drunk. When assured this was not the case, they were hailed as heroes and given all the vodka they could handle. As to the overall casualty

THE VICTORIA CROSS

The debacle that was the Charge of the Light Brigade resolved the Queen to institute the Victoria Cross as the first high-level award open to all ranks. The medal should only be struck from Russian guns captured in the Crimea (still the understanding of most when it comes to the VC medal). Unfortunately, this specificity failed to make it through to Woolwich Arsenal where, keen to be rid of a couple of broken Chinese guns, they hacked off the rear ends of these and sent the chunks of metal to Hancocks of London, the jewellers commissioned to strike the medals.

The first Crimean veterans to receive their medals lined up in Hyde Park on 26 June 1857 where, against all advice, Victoria dished out the gongs from horseback. Coming to the first of the sixty-two recipients, Lt Henry James Raby, she slipped in her side-saddle when leaning down and pinned the poor chap straight through the nipple with his VC. With the same fortitude that had placed him before the Queen that day, Raby reportedly neither flinched nor uttered a sound.

list, this was miraculously low given the circumstances. Only 110 were killed, 161 wounded and another 60 taken prisoner, with the most cogent comment on the fiasco coming from the observing French General Bosquet who, as the Light Brigade rode to the guns, opined: 'C'est magnifique mais ce n'est pas la guerre. C'est de la follie' (It's magnificent but it's not war. It's madness). But now it was time for the cover-up to begin.

Observing the folly unfold from his vantage point, Raglan was quick to realize that someone's head was going to roll and, determined it would not be his, he and Airey dispatched another galloper to retrieve the ridiculously worded order from Lord Lucan. Sir George Paget, commander of the 4th Light Dragoons, which had the misfortune to form one quarter of the Light Brigade, observed at the time that even had they attacked the Causeway Heights, as Raglan intended, their charge would still have ended in disaster – so why, he demanded to know, had such an incoherent and stupid order been given in the first place?

Unfortunately for Raglan and Airey, Lucan had also realized the potential significance of that scrap of paper, which he had given to his civilian interpreter, John Elijah Blunt, with instruction to keep it safe. Consequently, Raglan and Airey only ever saw the return of copies of their order despite their repeated demands for the return of the original. This gambit, however, sealed Lucan's fate. Blamed by Raglan for failing to clarify the order to Cardigan, he was returned to England in disgrace. In his absence, Nolan was blamed (with some justification) for his failure to clarify the order on delivery to Lucan. Raglan refused to be drawn on the subject while, feeling unfairly pilloried (again with some justification), Lucan demanded to be court-marshalled so he could give his account and present the original order. With Raglan such an important figure in the Establishment, his repeated requests were denied.

As *The Times* thundered that someone had blundered, the Establishment connived to envelop the event in the cloak of unquestioning heroism and, after Poet Laureate Alfred, Lord Tennyson published his rather mawkish 'The Charge of the Light Brigade' in December 1854, this was pretty much the way the British public chose to regard the folly. The use of war literature to glorify the inglorious tends to obscure the realities of the events they portray and, while weeping over music-hall recitations of Tennyson's ditty, the great British public studiously ignored the incredible hardship and poverty endured by the Crimean veterans in their very midst. So much so that in 1890 Rudyard Kipling felt it necessary to publish 'The Last of the Light Brigade', highlighting the bravery of the troops in the Crimea and the poverty of the survivors, to successfully goad the collective conscience into belated action.

<hr>

WHAT LIT THE GREAT FIRE OF
CHICAGO: COW OR COMET?

THE CITY OF Chicago was ravaged by a fire that broke out around 9 p.m. on the night of 8 October 1871. It ranks high on the list of urban conflagrations in the history of the United States: by the time the fire was on the wane nearly four square miles of the city had been razed to the ground, leaving up to 300 dead, over 100,000 homeless and a clean-up bill of $222 million, approximately $4.5 billion in today's money. Even before the embers had cooled, rumours were blaming the conflagration on the O'Leary family of DeKoven Street, claiming that the fire had been started in a barn to the rear of that property when a drunken Catherine O'Leary's ineptitude at the milking of her cow had caused the belligerent bovine to kick over a lamp she had carelessly left on the straw-strewn floor. No matter the early refutations of this maliciously inspired nonsense, the notion of a simple cow bringing down the city of Chicago gripped the collective imagination, with Brian Wilson writing his 'Mrs O'Leary's Cow' track for the Beach Boys' initially unreleased *Smile* album as recently as 1967.

One of the first fire outbreaks attended to that night was indeed at a barn to the rear of the O'Leary residence at

137 DeKoven Street. The fire marshal in attendance later testified: 'We got the fire under control and it would not have gone a foot further but the next thing I knew was that they came and told me that St Paul's Church, about two squares north, was on fire.' The team rushed to attend that event but, as that same fire marshal recalled, on arrival, 'The next thing I knew then was that the fire was over at Bateham's Planing Mill ... buildings far beyond the line of fire, and in no contact with it, burst into flames from the interior'. If nothing else, this fire marshal's testimony makes clear that the old legend of the disaster having been started by Catherine O'Leary's cow kicking over her lamp can be safely dismissed, especially as the journalist who first published the story would later have to admit to its invention. The Irish Catholic contingent of Chicago was not held in high regard by the Protestant elite so a scapegoat, or perhaps a scapecow, from that community fitted the bill nicely.

With history books very much focused on the Great Fire of Chicago, there was often little mention of the fact that this was not the only fire in the area of the American Great Lakes that night. The townships of Port Huron and White Rock, both at the southern end of Lake Huron, were pretty much wiped out the same night, as were those of Holland and Manistee on Lake Michigan. Across the lake from Manistee and Holland was the site of a fire so massive that it dwarfed all the others put together; the largely forgotten fire of Peshtigo, which killed around 2,500 people and destroyed a dozen surrounding villages and over 1.5 million acres of woodland. It was unquestionably the worst fire in American history – so how did all this get overshadowed by the Chicago fire?

At its peak, the Peshtigo fire presented the awesome sight of a towering wall of flame across a 5-mile front with temperatures exceeding 2,000°F, reaching speeds of over 100 mph. Trains were melted where they stood while buildings and their fleeing occupants were burned before the fire had even reached them. As was the case across the waters in Chicago, the Peshtigo event was marked by multiple and diverse fires which, erupting at random across a wide area, left the people at a loss as to the direction in which to flee. Many who sought sanctuary in the nearby rivers and lakes either drowned or died of hypothermia. The subsequent study of the fire, its prevailing conditions and the fire tornados it created produced what is still known as the Peshtigo Paradigm. A blueprint for how to reproduce the holocaustic conditions that wiped out Peshtigo, this study was used by the US Air Force and British Bomber Command to generate the fire storms in their Second World War incendiary bombing of Dresden and Tokyo, which inflicted death tolls to dwarf those of Hiroshima and Nagasaki combined.

The most intriguing aspect presented by this collection of fires is the fact that, when viewed from the air or plotted on a map, they present a spread pattern similar to a shotgun blast to a solid surface from a shallow angle. This led some to consider a culprit far more mysterious than Mother O'Leary's cow – the blistering hot debris falling from Biela's Comet, which also broke up over the area that night. First mooted in 1883, the comet theory was roundly dismissed, mainly because the man who put forward the theory was Ignatius Loyola Donnelly, a

THE MAKING OF THE O'LEARYS

Despite the rather obvious clue that their home had survived the catastrophe, the O'Learys' lives became unbearable as they were routinely beset by reporters and other more hostile mobs, all of which forced the family to decamp to the city's notorious Southside to avoid further persecution. In one of those strange twists of history, this enforced exile proved the making of the O'Leary family's fortunes and laid the foundations for Chicago's reputation in the field of organized crime. Within a few years of the family's move, Catherine's son, James, was running errands for the local bookmakers and organizing the violent extraction of monies due from punters reluctant to keep up their payments. By the opening of the 1900s, Big Jim O'Leary had carved out his empire of illegal gambling and racketeering and, a multimillionaire, he was one of the city's richest 'celebrities'. His partnership with syndicate boss Johnny Torrio took him to greater heights and set up Chicago as the ideal stage onto which would walk Torrio's 'lieutenant', Al Capone.

US congressman and amateur scientist widely perceived, with some justification, as a bit of a crank. In Donnelly's favour were the countless witness reports of balls of fire falling from the sky that night and spontaneous ground-level ignitions of blue flame, which Donnelly maintained were consistent with methane found in comets and comet debris. More recently, the American physicist Dr Robert Wood took up Donnelley's long-abandoned gauntlet and, in 2004, presented his conclusions to the American Institute of Aeronautics and Astronautics, asserting that there was, after all, much to support the notion that this cluster of fires had indeed been started by Biela's break-up showering the area with white-hot debris as this – and only this – squared with what so many eyewitnesses uniformly recalled at the time.

Soon after the fires came the publication of *The History of the Great Conflagration* (1871) by John Washington Sheahan and George Putnam Upton, two local historians who collected and meticulously logged locals' accounts of the night. They reported recollections of what happened in a village near Peshtigo:

But a few minutes after nine o'clock, and by a singular coincidence precisely the time at which the Chicago fire commenced, the people of the village heard a terrible roar. It was that of a tornado crashing through the forests. Instantly the heavens were illuminated with a terrible glare. The sky, which had been so dark a moment before, burst into clouds of flame. A spectator of the terrible events said the fire did not come upon them gradually from burning trees and other objects to the windward, but from a whirlwind of flames in great clouds from above the tops of the trees.

Others were equally adamant that the fire came 'in great sheeted flames *from* the heavens' and also spoke of 'a pitiless rain of fire and hot sand from the skies'. Many also spoke of 'great balls of fire falling from the sky. The whole sky was filled with them, great smoky masses about the size of a large balloon and travelling at unbelievable speed. They fell to the ground and burst.'

As to those mentions of searing hot sand, this was addressed in the book *Mrs O'Leary's Comet* (1985) by Mel Waskin, head writer and science producer for the Chicago-based Coronet Educational Films. Knowing that meteors can bring in their wake showers of silica, Waskin observed: 'There was sand on the beaches but the beaches lay to the east and the wind was blowing from the west and the south. There was no sand on the floor of the forests nor on the farmlands of Wisconsin.'

It is true that, in the main, debris from space is usually cold by the time it hits earth, and that many such visitors from space of modest size are destroyed by their passage through the earth's atmosphere, resulting in them falling as 'sand'. Other larger ones, however, have in the past and more recently made it through that barrier to inflict significant earth-impact with accompanying fires. On 29 August 2011 a single such object was observed leaving

THE MYSTERIES OF HISTORY

a flaming trail as it passed over the Peruvian city of Cusco to crash into the tinder-dry forests to the south of the city, immediately bursting into flames. Much the same happened on 11 August 2013 in the forests adjacent to the town of Kepez Çanakkale in Turkey. In a major event, such as the disintegration of Beila's Comet, hundreds or even thousands of individual pieces of varying size would have resulted, some burning up to fall as the much-cited hot sand at Peshtigo while larger ones made it to earth to start fires.

In 1893, the journalist Michael Ahern finally admitted his libel of the O'Learys' cow but by then no one was listening. At least Mrs O'Leary and her cow finally received official exoneration from the Chicago City Council which, in October 1997, held a somewhat belated and rather tongue-in-cheek ceremony. The cow, it was proclaimed, had been the victim of bad press.

<hr />

SUICIDE BY PROXY:
THE DEATH OF
GENERAL GORDON

BY ALL ACCOUNTS, Charles Gordon was a bit of an oddball. He was a Christian fundamentalist, whose faith sat in stern condemnation of his own homosexuality. Frequently writing and opining that he wished he had been born a eunuch, this internal strife likely lay at the core of his well-acknowledged death wish. While still aged twenty-two in 1855 he was detailed to the war against Russia being fought on the Crimean peninsula and so wrote to his sister, Augusta, that he was off to Balaklava, 'hoping, without having a hand in it, to be killed'. After rising meteorically through the ranks, Gordon would later be lionized by the British public for his suppression of the Taiping Rebellion (1850–64), a civil war that tore through China as the nationalistic Taipings, their name translating rather ironically as great peace, sought to bring down the ruling Manchu dynasty and replace it with what they called the Heavenly Kingdom. Hailed at home as 'Chinese' Gordon, he was not, understandably, held in such high regard in China, where he is still depicted as little more than an imperialist bully boy.

Returned from China, Gordon became morose and something of a recluse, with some suspicious of his motives for devoting so much of his time and money to running schools for homeless boys plucked from the London slums.

Gordon's self-imposed hermitage, however, was not destined to endure. Come 1883, Muhammad Ahmad, the self-proclaimed Mahdi (a sort of Islamic Messiah), had brought the Sudan to the brink of internecine conflict and the British public began calling for 'Chinese' Gordon to sort it all out. By January 1884, the Gladstone government had given in to this public demand and dispatched Gordon to Africa with strict orders to organize the evacuation of Khartoum but not to tarry a moment longer than was absolutely necessary. But the thing Gladstone feared most came to pass, with Gordon becoming entrenched and unable to leave the city.

Gladstone was unaware that Gordon had already resolved that he would never leave Khartoum; he had decided that the city would serve as the venue for his much-desired martyrdom. It has been suggested that Gordon, morose and introspective from his formative years, was afflicted by Asperger's syndrome; he was most certainly prone to protracted bouts of depressive self-examination during which he read nothing but the Bible. Sir Evelyn Baring, the British Consul-General of Egypt, reported back to Westminster that as Gordon seemed to take his instructions directly from the prophets of the Old Testament he would be unlikely in the extreme to follow the dictates of any mortal – and it seems Baring was right. As Gordon approached Khartoum he became increasingly messianic, proclaiming he would 'cast down the Mahdi' and his 'rabble of feeble stinking Dervishes', and sent telegrams to the city pronouncing 'Be not afraid. Ye are men, not women. I, Gordon, am coming.' And then, to make sure his own fate was sealed, having crossed the border into Sudan, Gordon held a meeting in the town of Berber, in northern Sudan, with local tribal leaders. He revealed to them the details of his secret orders to evacuate all British personnel from Khartoum as the Egyptians, who already had troops on Sudanese soil, had announced their impending withdrawal in the face of the Mahdi's escalating activity. In view of the fact that Gordon had already expressed the opinion that 'The moment it is known that we have given up the game every man will go over to the Mahdi', this move cannot be seen in any other light than a form of suicide.

Once ensconced in the city, Gordon made public his intention to hold out against the Mahdi before organizing the evacuation of nearly 3,000 non-combatants, which left him with about 8,000 well-armed troops, a massive stockpile of ammunition and adequate artillery. But it was only a matter of time; the Mahdi laid siege to the city in March 1884 and, by the close of that year, the population was starved close to death. Gordon wrote to his sister that he hoped it would be God's will for him to die there as 'Earth's joys grow very dim; its glories have faded.' He was incessantly chain-smoking and, when not attacking

his servants during his increasingly violent mood swings, he spent more time discussing God's mighty plans with the mouse that had taken up residence in his office than he did orchestrating the city's defences. Back in the UK, the public, unaware of Gordon's state of mind, attacked Gladstone for not sending a relief column to save its hero. Eventually, after Queen Victoria herself also demanded he did so, the prime minster had to relent and in August 1884 he appointed Field Marshal Sir Garnet Wolseley to lead the Nile Expedition, ordering him to make ready to march on Khartoum with all possible haste – and this is where Thomas Cook Travel came into the picture.

Born in Derbyshire in 1808, Thomas Cook was a

THE MAHDI

Within six months of his victory over Gordon at Khartoum, the Mahdi Muhammad Ahmad was himself dead from typhus. But the war he had started continued until Lord Kitchener arrived in the Sudan to conduct a vengeful campaign of such brutality that one of his young lieutenants, Winston Churchill, wrote an open condemnation of his 'kill-them-all' policy.

The only ammunition Kitchener took to the Sudan was the later-banned dum-dum round, a hollow-point bullet that 'mushroomed' on impact; he also had several of the Mahdi's sons and other relatives shot out of hand.

The Mahdi's surviving son, Sayidd al-Mahdi, born the year of his father's death, was later seen by the British as a moderate with whom they could do business. A measured and temperate man, he had meetings with King Farouk of Egypt, later opening up talks in the 1950s with British Foreign Secretary Sir Anthony Eden and Prime Minister Winston Churchill. A skilled negotiator, Sayidd al-Mahdi secured Sudanese independence from the Egyptian–British alliance on 1 January 1956.

dedicated temperance preacher organizing meetings and taking his congregation, as well as others, to listen to preachers at temperance rallies around the country. His first venture was a package deal with Midland Railways to round-trip 500 passengers to such a rally in Loughborough on 5 July 1841 at a shilling a head. By 1870 he was advertising round-the-world trips, which inspired Jules Verne to pen *Around the World in Eighty Days* (1873). He was also running archaeological trips up the Nile in agreement with various tribal leaders and local warlords along its banks to ensure free passage. Aware of Thomas Cook's corporate expertise in the movement of large numbers of people in foreign climes and anxious to move the Nile Expedition relief column as swiftly as possible, Gladstone hired Thomas Cook to handle the logistics, which must make Wolseley's army the first to have set out to war on a package holiday deal. Despite Cook's efficiency, the relief arrived just two days too late.

Overrun by the Mahdi's forces, almost everyone in the city had been slaughtered, including Gordon, whom survivors stated to have died ranting biblical passages and firing his revolver until cut down. His head was cut off and paraded in front of the victors on a pike before being jammed into the fork of a tree for the crows to pick at. The rest of his body was hacked up and thrown down a well. Naturally this was not something that Gladstone thought would go down well at home so a myth was circulated that Gordon had walked out unarmed to meet his death in full uniform, with the very sight of his serene calm causing the invading horde to fall back in awe – until one coward threw a spear at him. The artist George William Joy was commissioned to run up a canvas depicting this version of events, a propaganda coup that worked so well that this is still how most remember Gordon's death. Such was the public outpouring of grief over his passing that when a written rebuke from Queen Victoria, blaming Gladstone for Gordon's death, was made public, he was kicked out of office.

———◁◯▷———

THE BOMBING OF GUERNICA:
CAPTURING THE FALLING
SOLDIER

FOR MOST, THE bombing of Guernica and the photograph of the so-called Falling Soldier epitomized the horrors of the Spanish Civil War (1936–9). But did the reports of that bombing accurately reflect what really happened and was that photograph all it seemed?

That Guernica was the target of aerial bombardment on 26 April 1937 is beyond dispute, but the severity, duration and objective of the perpetrators are the subject of claim and counterclaim. The Communist-backed Republicans claim the town was obliterated after being bombed on a busy market day, resulting in thousands of deaths, while the Nationalists, led by the ultimately victorious General Franco, who was supported by Nazi Germany, asserted that the town was a legitimate target and the bombardment had been strategic and of limited severity. Again, according to the Republicans, the raid on the town, which the locals prefer to call Gernika, was carried out by the German Condor Legion – which never denied its involvement – with the allegedly dark objective of testing out the effectiveness of the pattern bombing of civilians in preparation for the forthcoming Second World War. In keeping with this hidden agendum, the Condor Legion, under the command of Wolfram von Richthofen, cousin of the more notorious Red Baron, selected the 'innocent' town of Guernica at random and cynically planned to bomb it to give their chap with the abacus the best chance of coming up with some impressive figures. Yet there is nothing to support this suggestion and much to contradict it.

The Republican forces in that area were in full retreat and, given the direction in which they were heading, it was obvious to everyone in the area that they would bottleneck at Guernica in the Basque province of Vizcaya, better known as Biscay to outsiders. The town also had a serviceable rail-head and was home to the Astra small-arms factory so it would have been something of a miracle had the place *not* been selected as a target. The day in question was a Monday which, under normal circumstances for Guernica, would have been a market day and thus a day resulting in an increased civilian presence, but markets had already been banned for their propensity to block up the roads. Even had this not been so, the rural population surrounding the town, noting the ever-increasing Republican presence, had already figured out for itself what was on the cards for Guernica and had resolved to give the place a very wide berth. The German objective, according to von Richthofen, was to take out the bridges and destroy the road infrastructure to restrict movement out of Guernica, as Nationalist forces on the ground were fast approaching the town.

The attack force comprised two Heinkel 111s, one Dornier 17, eighteen Junkers 52s and three Italian Savoia-Marchetti 79s, which between them carried 22 tons of 250 kg or 50 kg bombs and 1 kg incendiaries. The first of the five waves of attack came at 4.30 p.m. and was carried out by the DO 17, which approached the town from the south to drop twelve 50 kg bombs. Next came the Italian SM 79s with explicit orders to bomb the bridge and roads to the east of the town but not to bomb the town itself – a strange overrider to their orders had the obliteration of Guernica been the prime objective. There were three more waves involving the Heinkels and the Junkers with the last of these ceasing at about 6 p.m. when, according to some accounts, about a quarter of the town had either been flattened or was on fire. Smaller then than it is now, Guernica has never been a big place and most expert opinion agrees that this is about what one could have expected the German Army to achieve from the payload their planes were known to have been carrying. It should also be remembered that the bomb weights mentioned above reflect the overall weight of the ordnance dropped; on average the explosive payload of a 1930s bomb stood at something less than 50 per cent of the overall bomb weight, so the combined weight dropped was about 10 tons of explosives. Not pleasant if you are underneath it when it falls but this hardly constitutes a heavy bombardment in the context of war.

Naturally, the Republicans of the time maintained that over half the town had been destroyed but, if that was true and the total obliteration of Guernica had been the objective, why didn't the Germans simply mount another air raid of similar strength to achieve that alleged objective? And if over half the town was in ruins, as the Republicans maintained, why is much of Guernica's early architecture still standing today? The nineteenth-century parliament buildings are still there, as is the Tribunales, the fifteenth-century Church of Santa Maria and the thirteenth-century Church of St Thomas. And what of the death toll? Again, and as one would expect, the Republicans trumpeted that over 2,000 innocent civilians had been killed, but that is quite impossible. The average kill rate inflicted by 1930s aerial bombardment on free-running ground personnel in an urban location was about seven deaths per ton of ordnance dropped. Seven times 22 (tons) is 154, which fits neatly with the more accurate body count of 153 established by the Gernikazarra Historia Taldea (Gernikazarra History Group) soon after the event. Yet this quiet voice of sanity has failed to stifle claims still coming from both sides of the argument. As late as 30 January 1970, the pro-Franco Madrid-based newspaper, *Arriba*, stated that there were only twelve deaths in Guernica that day, a claim as ridiculous as those from the pro-Republican camp maintaining a death toll running into the thousands.

Cold War spy Kim Philby, whose left-wing sympathies for the Russian-backed Republicans can hardly be questioned in the light of later revelations, is known to have been in Guernica on 28 April. Already in Moscow's

ENFANTS PERDUS

The Spanish Civil War began on 18 July 1936 when the Hitler–Mussolini-backed General Franco mounted a coup against the Communist-backed Republican government. Only from a distance did the Republican cause look like the romantic adventure it was depicted to be by the likes of Ernest Hemingway who, for all his later tales of derring-do, spent most of his time in Madrid's Hotel Florida, drinking and filing copy based on second-hand information.

Most of the idealistic foreigners who flooded to the Republican banner soon saw the harsh realities of the war. Nearly 3,000 Americans joined the Lincoln Battalion but, under Republican commanders, they were simply used as '*enfants perdus*' to attack enemy positions too well entrenched to risk fully trained Spanish troops. By the time the battalion decided to go home in 1938, over a third were either dead or seriously injured. It was much the same for other International Brigades which, collectively numbering 60,000, were likewise depleted by over a third through the same cynical misuse.

pocket, he had been ordered by Stalin to organize the assassination of Franco. Some of his clandestine activities aroused the suspicions of Reuters correspondent Ernest

Sheepshanks, a threat Philby allegedly removed by tossing a grenade into his car. Be that as it may, his copy filed to *The Times* that day read:

> It is feared that the conflagration destroyed much of the evidence of its origin, but it is felt here that enough remains to support the Nationalist contention that incendiaries on the Basque side had more to do with the razing of Guernica than did General Franco's aircraft. Few fragments of bombs have been recovered, the facades of buildings still standing are unmarked and the few craters I inspected were larger than anything hitherto made by any bomb in Spain. From their positions (most corresponded to the known location of manholes in the roads) it is a fair inference that these craters were caused by exploding mines which were unscientifically laid to cut roads. In view of these circumstances it is difficult to believe that Guernica was the target of bombardment of exceptional intensity by the Nationalists or an experiment with incendiary bombs, as is alleged by the Basques.

Others took pictures of buildings that had quite obviously been torched from the inside with the abandoned petrol containers still scattered about in evidence. True, the Condor Legion dropped a limited number of lightweight incendiaries, each with a payload of about 450 g but, by the very nature of their delivery, these tend to burn multistorey buildings from the top down and most of the burnt-out shells of buildings inspected shortly after the raid had burned from the bottom up. Many of the foreign journalists who visited the town after the raid seem to have been of the opinion that it would have taken many hundreds of bombs to achieve the level of destruction that confronted them. Most suspicious of all was the fact that, with Guernica once the capital of the Basque lands, the quarter of the town where still stands the old Meeting House and the sacred oak, *Gernikako Arbola* (The Tree of Guernica), under which the Council of Vizcaya first received its Royal Charters of Privilege in the Middle Ages, was completely unscathed. The spiritual and historic importance of this unscathed part of the town to Basques does raise a rather large question mark over who did what to Guernica.

But no matter, the Republicans won the propaganda war by commissioning Picasso to run up his still-famous *Guernica* which, measuring about 12 feet by 25 feet, presents the viewer with nightmare images and made its debut in the Spanish Pavilion at the 1937 World's Fair. A picture, they say, is worth a thousand words and Picasso's painting spoke volumes on the very real horrors of the Spanish Civil War to other countries – especially the USA, which somehow managed to utter eloquent condemnation of the war in general and the bombing of Guernica in particular while remaining tight-lipped about the American pilots involved in the first-ever concentrated bombing of civilians in a wholly innocent town. Helping the Spanish put down the Berber uprising in Morocco in 1925, an American-staffed squadron bombed the insignificant town of Chefchaouen to inflict staggering casualties. Of no military significance whatsoever and a town of about the same size as Guernica – with a population of perhaps 7,000 – the town was hit for no other reason than to break the will of the insurgents. As they say in that Moroccan town, 'everyone in Chefchaouen has heard of Guernica but no one in Guernica has heard of Chefchaouen'.

It is probably fair to say that few books or films fail to depict members of the Franco–German forces as cardboard cut-out fascist baddies and the Republicans as noble idealists struggling against a determined and sadistic opposition. Rarely is there any mention of the 50,000 civilian murders committed by those noble idealists who were every bit as enthusiastic in their atrocities as the Nationalists. As good communists, the Republicans harboured a particular hatred for the Church, resulting in some 7,000 clerics and nuns being variously raped, crucified, thrown to the bulls in the arenas, burned alive or castrated and thrown down wells in the hope of poisoning the local water supply. One of the most ardent cleric killers was a woman known only as La Pecosa, or the Freckled One, who seems to have taken particular delight in organizing the gang rape of nuns prior to their execution. On the night of 19 July 1936, Republican militia went on the rampage in Barcelona to torch fifty of the city's churches, leaving only eight others and the cathedral standing. In the Aragon city of Barbastro over 90 per cent of the clergy were murdered and about 62 per cent in the city of Lérida; Tortosa in Catalonia, Segorbe in Valencia, Málaga, Minorca and Toledo escaped with a mere 50 per cent cull of their clerics. As is ever the case in such internecine conflict, no one emerged with clean hands.

On 5 September 1936, the man born Endre Friedmann, who was destined to achieve international fame as a war correspondent and photographer under the pseudonym of Robert Capa, claimed to have been outside the village of Cerro Muriano in the province of Córdoba when he fortuitously snapped a Republican militiaman in the instant he was shot in the head by a distant sniper. The image became an overnight icon with the young man falling back, arms spread and his rifle falling from his dead, right hand. Still a popular wall-poster, Capra's snap went unchallenged until 1975 when Spanish geographers and historians took a closer look at both the central figure and the configuration of the landfall in the background. The so-called Falling Soldier was allegedly Federico Borrell García, an anarchist volunteer, but suspicions were first aroused by the fact that, although he was indeed killed outside Cerro Muriano on 5 September 1936, all his comrades were united in their reports that he had been shot while taking cover behind a tree. Not only are trees conspicuously absent from the peripheral terrain in Capa's photograph but Capa himself was not recorded as having been in the area at the time.

On the geographical front, the configuration of the hinterlands in the distant background bears no relationship to any eyeline taken from anywhere around Cerro Muriano. According to José Manuel Susperregui Etxebeste, Professor of Audiovisual Communications at the University of the Basque Country, who has written much on the photographic legacy of the conflict, the photograph matches identically the geographical skyline at Espejo, some 30 miles to the south-east of Cerro Muriano. In 1936, the only fighting around that town took place on the 22 and 25 September, by which time García was some three weeks dead and Capa, again, was not in the area. It seems that the photograph cannot have been of García and cannot have been taken in Cerro Muriano. Etxebeste further states that the photograph must have been taken several weeks before Capa's claimed date and not with his famed Leica, but with the Rolleiflex of his then lover and business partner, Gerda Taro, and that said camera must have been mounted on a tripod at the time. In other words, the whole thing had been staged.

No matter where it was staged or whether it was Capa or Taro who clicked the shutter, that photograph will doubtless retain its iconic status. The Italians have a saying, '*Se non e vero, e ben trovato*', or 'If it isn't true it is well invented' – and the Capa snap is nothing if not '*ben trovato*'.

ACKNOWLEDGEMENTS

With special thanks to Dr Karl Kruszelnicki of the Physics Department of the University of Sidney, who was kind enough to take the time to explain to me in person just why any celestial or solar alignments that may occur today at Stonehenge would not have done so 5,000 years ago.

BIBLIOGRAPHY

Alexander, Caroline; *The Bounty: The True Story of the Mutiny on the Bounty*, Harper Perennial, 2004

Baring-Gould, Sabine; *Curious Myths of the Middle Ages*, Dover Publications, 2005 (originally published 1866)

Boureau, Alain, Lydia G. Cochrane (trans.); *The Myth of Pope Joan*, University of Chicago Press, 2001

Bradbury, Jim; *Robin Hood: The Real Story of the English Outlaw*, Amberley Publishing, 2012

Brooks, Polly Schoyer; *Beyond the Myth: The Story of Joan of Arc*, Houghton Mifflin, 1999

Davidovitz, Joseph; *Why the Pharaohs Built the Pyramids with Fake Stones*, Geopolymer Institute of France, 2004

Gies, Frances; *Joan of Arc: The Legend and the Reality*, Harper Perennial, 1981 (originally published 1842)

Holmes, Rachel; *Scanty Particulars: The Life of Dr James Barry*, Penguin, 2003

Kamen, Henry; *The Spanish Inquisition: A Historical Revision*, Yale University Press, 2014

Kawashima, Yasuhide; *The Tokyo Rose Case: Treason on Trial*, University Press of Kansas, 2013

Menzies, Gavin and Ian Hudson; *Who Discovered America? The Untold History of the Peopling of the Americas*, William Morrow, 2014

Murray, Thomas; *The Story of the Irish in Argentina*, Forgotten Books, 2017 (originally published 1919)

Du Preez, Michael and Jeremy Dronfield; *Dr James Barry: A Woman Ahead of Her Time*, Oneworld Publications, 2017

Rennison, Nick; *Robin Hood: Myth, History and Culture*, Pocket Essentials, 2012

Rose, June; *The Perfect Gentleman: Dr James Miranda Barry*, Hutchinson, 1977

Smith, Douglas; *Rasputin: The Biography*, Pan Macmillan, 2017

Smith, Michael; *Six: The Real James Bonds 1909-1939*, Biteback Publishing, 2011

Suchet, John; *Mozart: The Man Revealed*, Elliott & Thompson, 2016

Turnbull, Stephen; *Ninja: Unmasking the Myth*, Frontline Books, 2017

Turnbull, Stephen; *Warriors of Medieval Japan*, Osprey Publishing, 2005

Wilson-Smith, Timothy; *Joan of Arc: Maid, Myth and History*, The History Press, 2008

Wood, Frances; *Did Marco Polo Go to China?*, Martin Secker & Warburg, 1996

Young, Rosalind; *Mutiny of the Bounty and Story of Pitcairn Island 1790–1894*, University Press of the Pacific, 2003 (originally published 1894)

INDEX